Parenting Middle Schoolers Made Easy

Empower Your Tween With Strong Self-Confidence, High Emotional Intelligence, and Essential Skills to Thrive in School and Life

Grace A. Clark

First edition

CONTENTS

INTRODUCTION

P arenting is undeniably one of life's most formidable challenges. Responsibilities multiply from the time a child is born. This role is not limited to physical care; it encompasses the emotional burden of ensuring a child's future, safety, and happiness and the mental pressure of being a role model to our child. Bob Keeshan stated, "Parents are the ultimate role models for children. Every word, movement, and action has an effect. No other person or outside force has a greater influence on a child than a parent."

Navigating the developmental stages of a child's life, particularly the tween years — ages 10 to 13 — is incredibly daunting. This critical period is characterized by profound physical, mental, and emotional changes as children begin to assert their independence, confront the complexities of middle school, and tackle pressures within and beyond their control.

Middle school serves as a crucial foundation for academic achievement and the development of lifelong habits. Yet, this transition is riddled with challenges as tweens vacillate between seeking autonomy and requiring guidance, all against the backdrop of hormonal upheaval.

Though invaluable, the plethora of parenting advice from child psychologists and educators can sometimes seem impractical for daily application. My own experiences, shaped by a childhood in the Midwest of the US with hardworking but often absent parents, led to an intense involvement in my children's education. I was driven by a desire to provide the nurturing and support I missed, constantly searching for the ideal school setting to foster my children's growth and safety.

My eldest child attended six different schools from age 4 to 13, from a Montessori kindergarten promoting individualized learning but lacking in time management concept through a spectrum of public, charter, and private schools, each with unique challenges, including a small, nurturing Christian middle school offering closer attention yet limited social interactions. And I have tried homeschooling, too. When my eldest entered a large public high school, he struggled with the lack of individualized learning and not knowing anyone on a big campus, but soon, he demonstrated the resilience he had developed over frequently changing learning environments over the years.

My eldest child's educational path reflects my unyielding pursuit of a perfect learning environment. This relentless quest was rooted in my fear of failure as a parent and my reluctance to acknowledge my role in a cycle of continual dissatisfaction. Recognizing myself as the common factor in these challenges was pivotal in my parenting journey. Interacting with a diverse array of parents across various schools and sharing frustrations and solutions about raising tweens provided invaluable insights and mutual support, which led me to self-discovery and helped me refine my approach to parenting.

Inspired by these encounters and the education journey of my eldest, I adapted these insights for my younger children, leading to a significantly smoother experience for our entire family, which also inspired me to create a practical guide tailored to address the unique challenges of parenting middle schoolers.

What Sets this Book Apart?

In the sea of parenting books, you will find some are more clinically oriented, some are more specialized in one or two areas, and some are high-level but seem to be a kitchen sink of everything. I want to cut to the chase, save you time, and declutter your busy life with easily applicable tips you can apply the second you finish reading each tip. I have read many books, consulted professionals and educators, and researched parents' and children's behaviors. This book is a culmination of key learnings from many wonderful resources and the real-life experiences of many parents with whom I have crossed paths.

I break down complex or big concepts into simple layman's terms so you can read and apply them simultaneously. "Simplicity is the ultimate sophistication," according to DaVinci. Often, the simple things we do can make a big difference in our lives.

How to Use This Book?

The book consists of five parts. I arranged the content in a particular sequence so that earlier chapters were the foundation for making parenting middle schoolers easier. Common parenting headaches include children's mood swings, irrational or rebellious behaviors, low self-esteem and self-confidence, emotional outbursts, device addiction, lack of motivation, and lack of social skills, which are outer reflections of their inner struggles.

Instead of fighting with children's outer behavior issues, this book gives simple and practical tips to get to the root of the problems. You can incorporate the strategies and tips in the book into your daily life to help keep your sanity and rediscover joy in parenting. Taking different children's behaviors and family situations into consideration, each section offers different approaches and multiple tips. You can pick and choose to apply a subset of the tips or all of them based on your specific situations at home. You can treat some tips as sources of inspiration and customize them to fit your particular needs.

Part 5 discusses additional tips for challenging life circumstances, such as raising children during and after divorce or separation, children who need special learning accommodations, and navigating homeschooling. But if you read and practice the fundamentals, strategies, and tips discussed in Parts 1, 2, 3, and 4, you are already in a great position to tackle these circumstances. These additional insights and tips can further ease your parenting journey.

This guide is designed to address common parenting hurdles without being prescriptive, recognizing the distinctiveness of each child and family situation. It's not a manual you need to memorize but a companion to consult, offering step-by-step advice to revisit as needed. Through this approach, I aim to provide a resource that makes your parenting job easier, making your parenting experience manageable and enriching for the entire family. Let's get started!

PART 1. FOUNDATIONAL PREPARATION

CHAPTER 1: PRIORITIZE YOUR SELF-CARE

"When you take care of yourself, you're a better person for others. When you feel good about yourself, you treat others better."

— Solange Knowles

B eing a parent of tweens is an exciting but equally challenging journey that requires good mental and physical health. Before we discuss parenting strategies, let's first discuss the significance of prioritizing self-care for good parenting. Undoubtedly, there are many excellent nutrition, health, and fitness books. However, none focuses on parenting, along with physical and mental health at the same time. With this book, I want to discuss self-care in the context of parenting. I will highlight and simplify key actionable strategies you can apply immediately to nurture your physical, mental, and emotional health. The primary purpose is to help you get on the ladders of being a successful and happy parent of a tween.

Take Care of Your Physical Well-Being

First and foremost, your capacity to parent successfully depends on your physical well-being. Hence, you need to focus and prioritize your physical self-care by considering the following essential and proven strategies:

1. **Nourish Your Body with Quality Nutrients:** Consuming foods high in nutrients gives your body the strength and energy it needs to function. Choose a diet high in proteins, minerals, vitamins, and fiber and moderate in healthy fats and carbs. Also, remember to manage your total calorie intake and maintain a healthy weight and body mass index (BMI) range.

2. **Continue to Move Your Body:** Being physically active is equally im-

portant. Regular exercise five times a week will improve your mood, reduce stress, and increase your energy level. Now, it is entirely up to you which exercises you want to choose. You can start with yoga, hit the gym, go for a walk, or even indulge in some sports-related activities with your tween—the key point is to keep your body on the move.

3. **Obtain Enough and Quality Sleep:** People often take it for granted, but getting proper sleep is very important. Make getting quality sleep a priority to rejuvenate your body and mind. If you don't get enough sleep, meaning less than seven hours a day, you risk many health issues like weight gain, high BMI, diabetes, high blood pressure, heart disease, stroke, and depression. So, try to fix your sleep cycle immediately.

4. **Do Preventative Care:** With constant advancements in the medical and technology fields, many chronic illnesses and types of cancers can be prevented or caught earlier. Hence, it is better to take preventative measures to address health issues and rising costs effectively. Many people skip annual checkups and rob themselves of some early diagnosis and treatments. So, don't procrastinate on your yearly checkups; seek preventive care without procrastination.

Take Care of Your Mental Well-Being.

Having tweens, especially in middle school, can be mentally demanding. It requires tolerance, fortitude, and flexibility. So, with such great demands, it can be challenging to look after your well-being. But you don't have to worry as I am briefly highlighting some proven, key strategies to nurture and maintain your mental well-being while looking after your tween:

1. **Put Mindfulness into Practice:** Practice mindfulness exercises like deep breathing, meditation, visualization, positive affirmations, and journaling. It can help you develop mindfulness, gain peace of mind, manage stress, and stay in the present moment.

2. **Don't Battle Negative Thoughts:** Whenever negative thoughts come up, don't fight them; simply acknowledge them. One trick I learned from experienced meditation practitioners is to focus on and count breaths. For example, count to 5 while breathing in, count to 5 to hold the breath, and then count to 5 while breathing out. Keep repeating the counting until random thoughts go away.

3. **Establish Boundaries:** To avoid burnout and preserve a good balance, clearly define the boundaries between your personal and family

responsibilities. When it's necessary, practice saying no and give mental replenishment top priority.

4. **Seek Assistance:** Don't be afraid or shy to ask for help when you feel overwhelmed. Have a solid support system, whether via friends, family, or parent networks. It takes a village to raise a child, so leverage available resources in your community or online to keep your sanity.

5. **Overcome Perfectionism**: As parents, we try our best to take care of our children, but for some people, myself included at one point, we try to perfect everything, which can be mentally exhausting. Perfection is highly subjective and relative; the additional energy and time we put into perfecting something can yield a diminishing return. So, it is better to be yourself and never let the chains of perfectionism lock you.

6. **Continue to Enrich Your Mind:** Knowledge is power, especially in a fast-changing world. Learning and enriching your mind intellectually or spiritually can sharpen your mind and benefit your tween. You are enriching your mind now by reading this book.

Take Care of Your Emotional Well-Being.

Parenting tweens often involves navigating a rollercoaster of emotions, from joy and pride to frustration and worry. It can sometimes be hard to transition from emotions, so here are some key strategies to cultivate and safeguard your emotional well-being. It will help you stay calm and patient with your tween.

1. **Practice Self-Compassion:** Be kind to yourself and recognize that parenting is a journey of ups and downs. Embrace imperfection when things don't go as planned. Don't be too critical of yourself; focus on finding solutions and moving forward.

2. **Compartmentalize Feelings:** We are human and feel all kinds of feelings—good and bad. However, it is not easy to make your negative feelings disappear immediately, but you can practice compartmentalizing them. This enables you to decide where you want to put your energy at the moment, focusing on emotions that you feel necessary. It does take some practice, but you will get there.

3. **Engage in Activities You Enjoy:** Take time for activities that bring you joy and fulfillment outside your parenting role. Whether pursuing a hobby, indulging in a favorite pastime, or spending time in nature, prioritize activities that nourish your soul and take a break from emotional

shackles.

4. **Make Quality Social Connections:** Your social circle tends to change after you have children. It's easy to get bogged down by daily parenting commitments and start losing social connections. Humans, even introverts, have the basic need to socialize with others. So, stay connected to your good old friends, whether they are single or have children in different age groups.

5. **Avoid or Remove Toxic Connections:** Not everyone in your life is your well-wisher, so it is better to know how everyone feels about you and remove toxic people from your life. I know it's not easy to cut someone out of your life, but sometimes you have to - for your own good, as being with them does more harm than good.

Another common strategy to improve physical, mental, and emotional well-being simultaneously is to take breaks throughout the day and go on vacations or staycations (if on budget) several times a year to rejuvenate yourself. Taking short or longer breaks can give you new perspectives. So, always take breaks between work and throughout the day. Plan some vacations to get out of the current stresses of life and breathe the fresh air of serenity for your own tranquility.

When prioritizing your self-care, you invest in your well-being and lay the foundation for being the best parent you can be for your tween. And it certainly does not make you selfish when you focus on self-care. Airlines require each person to wear an oxygen mask before helping anyone else. It's the same logic: if we struggle to breathe and survive, we can't help others effectively. So, remember, by nurturing yourself, you're better equipped to nurture others. In the following chapters, I will go into more detail on the specifics of what parents can do to help cultivate tweens' physical, mental, and emotional health.

Key Takeaways:

- Taking care of your physical, mental, and emotional well-being is not a luxury but a necessity.

- Investing in ourselves helps increase resilience and mental clarity.

- Self-care gives parents more capacity to nurture and support our children with strength and grace.

If you prioritize self-care, you are ready to embark on this rewarding parenting path. Let's first understand or remind ourselves of the changes that tweens go through. Then, I will share simple strategies on how you can easily be there for your child.

Chapter 2: Understand Changes Your Middle Schoolers Go Through

"I go between wanting you to be my baby forever and being excited about all the amazing things you'll do in this life."

— Anonymous

D o you remember the fun days when your child was younger, making a mess and busy putting crayons in their mouths? Don't worry — those good old days aren't gone — they're just different. In this growing phase, your child is constantly changing. They are trying to figure out who they are in a world of peer pressure and social media. Everywhere they turn, someone tells them how to be cool, what their body shapes should be, and what is trending on social media.

Middle school is a magical time in your child's life. They are changing physically, mentally, and emotionally. It is during this time that puberty hits – that fun time when your son's voice changes or your daughter starts to have curves. Their emotions are everywhere, and they experience frequent mood changes. One minute, they are sweet; the next, they are on a rampage, determined to mess with your sanity, your house, and anything else that gets in their way. Welcome to parenting during the puberty phase. Since we can't avoid challenges, let's embrace challenges with a deeper understanding and apply effective strategies.

Physical and Emotional Development During Middle School

Every baby walks, talks, and is potty trained at their own pace; tweens (children ages ten through thirteen) and young teenagers go through puberty on their own schedule. On top of their outer physical changes, their hormones are going crazy. Their hormones affect how they feel about themselves, their world, and their friends and family. And because of hormones, mood changes can seem erratic. Hormones can make your child interested in sexuality, which can be a terrifying thought to many parents.

Physical Changes During Puberty

As children experience physical changes, many middle schoolers find themselves dealing with issues like body image, self-confidence, and just fitting in. Some children experience physical changes over a few weeks, while others take their time. You can show your children physiology-related educational videos and content. You can even share your own experiences by telling them stories about you, such as when your voice changed or when you first started your period. They might say, "Oooh, gross" or "TMI" (too much information), but you have opened the door for your child to come to you if they have questions or concerns.

Whether you know these already or not, I summarize some key changes that your child goes through during this phase of their life below because these are inevitable discussion topics that you will have with your child:

Girls

- Growth spurts — Girls tend to grow faster than boys.

- Breast Development — Girls develop breasts at different times. Sometimes, one breast can grow faster than the other. The process can be uncomfortable and even painful.

- Curves — Your daughter's body shape will change as her hips widen.

- Body hair growth — Pubic and armpit hair will start to grow, and so will the leg hair.

- Menstruation — Some girls will start with light periods, while others will have a heavy period their first time. Be prepared for either scenario.

- Additional changes — Due to their increased estrogen (hormone) levels, girls will experience vaginal discharge. Acne starts popping up.

Boys

- Growth spurt — Boys grow taller and have broad shoulders earlier than girls. Sometimes, their feet, arms, and legs grow faster than the rest of their bodies, making them feel awkward and clumsy.

- Genital growth — Their external genitals will grow. Sometimes, one of their testes may grow faster than the other.

- Body hair growth — They also experience pubic and armpit hair growth.

- Some degree of breast enlargement — Boys can experience slight breast development due to fluctuating hormone levels. It is usually temporary and will resolve on its own as their hormone level becomes more stable.

- Additional changes — As their testosterone increases, they might experience random and unexpected erections and ejaculations. Acne starts popping up.

Cultivate a Positive Self-Image

When your child is going through such changes, they must know you are there for them. There are several ways that you can guide your child to embrace and celebrate their self-image:

1. Remind them to accept their body types and celebrate who they are as a whole person.

2. Be mindful of how you talk about food. Address it as healthy vs. unhealthy.

3. Refrain from using words like "fat" or "thin" or commenting on other people's bodies.

4. Discuss what is real and fake (e.g., people use filters or photoshop to make their skin and bodies look perfect).

5. Help your child choose clothes that fit them comfortably.

6. Model positive self-image by listing positive qualities of yourself and your child and avoid comparing with others

Demonstrate Your Understanding Through Relatability

As much as it is crucial to cultivate a positive mindset in your children, it is equally important to help them understand through relatability and practical examples. Here's a list of ways through which you can help them:

1. Let your child know that you are ready to talk whenever they are.

2. Address your child's questions about sex and sexuality honestly using

language they can understand.

3. Acknowledge their curiosity. Don't ignore or embarrass them when they ask questions.

4. Look for natural conversation openers. Ask your child what they are thinking and feeling.

5. Be transparent and clear about everything, even if it doesn't align with your perspective.

Understand Middle Schoolers' Emotional Rollercoasters

Your child will likely experience a roller coaster of emotions during this phase. It is a difficult time for your adolescent as they try to figure out who they are and their place in the world. They would form relationships (even romantic ones) and gain some independence. So, it is essential to understand their wild roller coaster ride of emotions. Below are key things to keep in mind when you try to understand your child's emotional fluctuations:

1. It is important to recognize and accept your children's emotions.

2. Be understanding if they avoid talking. It's not about you; they need a little space.

3. When they do talk to you, validate their feelings.

4. Always let them know they have a right to feel whatever they feel. Please give them the space to sort through their emotions.

How to Handle Your Child's Emotions

It's easy to get frustrated with your child, but that is where things get edgy, and you might feel that you lose the grip of parenting. You need to be more flexible and approachable. Below are tips to help you handle your child's emotions with ease:

1. Breathe, stay calm, and be an active listener. Let your child express themselves without judging them, and always validate their feelings.

2. Ask questions about what they are feeling and why they are going through those particular emotions,

3. Just let them feel you are taking an interest in their life.

4. If either or both of you start to argue and get angry, take a break and talk about the situation after you cool off.

5. Try to figure out what sets them off and help them learn to cope with the situation. Please get to know your child's friends and make them feel welcome. Please invite them for dinner, offer to take them to the movies, or host a movie night.

6. Please help your child manage their responsibilities. If they become too overwhelmed, help them decide what to cut back on or eliminate.

7. Make time for family. Have a family night where everyone watches movies or plays board games. Schedule a time for bike riding, hiking, or zoo.

Key Takeaways

- Everyone experiences puberty differently. Everyone changes at different times.

- Let your child know that you are there for them.

- Answer all questions openly and honestly, using age-appropriate language and terms (even if they have heard it from social media and their friends).

- Actively listen to your child. Validate their feelings.

- Take some time for the family to have fun.

Now that you have a better handle on your child's emotions, I will discuss how you can help your child boost their self-confidence and resilience so they can self-regulate their emotions to some extent and make your parenting job easier.

Part 2. Empower Your Child with Self-Confidence

CHAPTER 3: FOSTER INDEPENDENCE AND SELF-CONFIDENCE

"One of the best parts of becoming a young adult is the freedom to stretch your wings. However, one of the hardest things about becoming a young adult is that your freedom requires responsibility. If you want to soar, it's up to you to look after yourself and to make choices that will keep you on your path."

— *Truth Be Told Quotes*

As you gain more understanding of the changes that your child is going through, let's talk about fostering your child's independence while setting the proper boundaries. Your child has been practicing independence since they started crawling. Their curiosity pushes those little beings to move and learn to gain control over their bodies. Most of their childhood is spent exploring new things, whether scooting a little, grabbing their favorite toy, or climbing on a chair to get a cookie, while the parents just run after them. However, as they get older, their independence takes a different turn, from just playing with other children in the neighborhood to wanting to go out with friends. It's natural for them to want to try things they have never done before.

During this phase of exploration and navigation, some tweens are less self-confident than others. They aren't sure whether they are good enough or smart enough, and some struggle with their body image. Although it is normal for your child to feel this way, you can help them overcome these self-doubts and boost their confidence. You can help your child become more independent and self-confident in multiple ways.

Promote Independence and Responsibility

You might be a little sad when your child pulls away from you and establishes their place in the world. Your tween has a busier life once they start middle school, with friends, clubs, sports, and other activities. You might feel relieved that you can have some free time but feel left out simultaneously. Although it might even hurt a little, their desire for independence is a positive sign of growth.

Your child has had some responsibilities since they were young, whether picking up their toys, brushing their teeth, or washing their hands before dinner. Each act signified learning and growth. Their responsibilities changed as they got older. They might be responsible for walking the dog, helping with dinner, and doing other chores. They also have academic responsibilities. In addition, they have new commitments and friendships to maintain. It's a lot to deal with, and while handling it all at once, many children distance themselves a little from their parents, which is entirely normal.   Please encourage them to be more independent and responsible at the same time. Below is a list of critical methods you can use partially or fully as you deem fit without overwhelming yourself.

1. Encourage your child to participate in activities outside of the home. This could mean joining clubs or playing sports.

2. Help them identify things they are interested in that will teach them new skills and abilities without forcing it upon them.

3. Please make time to connect with your child and let them know that you are there for them. Specifically, besides doing drop-off and pick-up for extracurricular activities, show interest in what their activities are.

4. Please encourage them to make good decisions.

5. Give your child some time freedom, but do set expectations on time limits (e.g., how much screen time per day or week). Discuss acceptable and unacceptable behaviors to give them freedom within boundaries.

6. Revisit expectations if your child takes their newly gained time freedom to the other end of the spectrum (e.g., exceeding their screen time limits) and explain the importance of following through with their words and making responsible choices.

7. Respect your middle schoolers' opinions and indulge with them more, catering to their queries.

8. Give your child space and respect their privacy.

9. Please encourage them to volunteer with a cause they support.

Teaching Personal Responsibility and Decision Making

Taking responsibility is essential for your child to grow and flourish in the real world. Once they take personal responsibility, they will be motivated to be accountable for their actions. Furthermore, they will develop empathy for others and can manage their time properly with self-discipline.

Here are some proven methods for teaching your middle schooler how to become more responsible. Again, you can choose which methods from this toolbox to use based on your child's behavior and bandwidth. Please don't feel compelled to use all of these methods at once.

1. Set reasonable expectations for what your child commits to doing (e.g., watering house plants three times a week, spending up to four hours a week gaming).

2. Give them chores to do every week. Please encourage your child to help even when they might not think it's their job.

3. Gradually increase the amount of responsibility that your child has based on how well they fulfill their existing commitments.

4. Let your child be responsible for their own choices. Equally important, ensure they know there must be consequences if they make irresponsible choices or intentionally make mistakes (e.g., hiding their gaming apps behind their homework browsers, joining unsupervised social media channels, etc.)

5. Trust your child to make good decisions, don't try to micromanage them unless they ask for help, and embrace their mistakes.

6. Give your child a chance to work out their own problems (Chapter 4 discusses this topic further).

7. Reward your child for being responsible and making good decisions.

8. Expose them to ways of making money and spending responsibly (more on this topic in Chapter 8 - Essential Life Skills). Explain the difference between needs and wants.

9. Volunteering is another way to teach responsibility and give back.

10. Please encourage them to be leaders once they join clubs, sports, or other youth groups.

11. Model responsibility and accountability. Talk about your responsibilities and your child's responsibilities often.

12. Accept their individualities and their opinions, even if it causes disagreement.

13. Help them set goals and encourage them to achieve them (more on this topic in Chapter 9, Time Management and Goal Setting).

Help Your Child Boost Self-Esteem and Self-Identity

It can be a challenging time for your child regarding self-esteem. Two of the main reasons are social media and peer pressure. They will see their peers in person and many images of strangers on the internet, and they feel conscious about looking different from others in their minds. So, they often start comparing themselves to others. This comparison is not just limited to looks but also to how others dress, how athletic they are, their grades, and a million other things. Comparison with others is what often lowers one's self-esteem.

Self-identity is another issue affected by social media and peers. Adolescence is when middle schoolers are trying to figure out who they are. It is easy for tweens to be confused by influencers on social media as they struggle to fit in.

Nurture a Healthy Self-Image

During puberty, your child might be more sensitive to their self-image. One child might eat like a horse and look thin, while another strives to eat healthy and looks curvier than they would like. Then, there are other issues that your child might feel self-conscious about, like hair, acne, braces, glasses, and a hundred different aspects of their physical appearance.

And your child could also be self-conscious about their abilities and compare themselves with their peers. One student might be exceedingly athletic and excel at every sport they try. Another student may get straight A's without trying hard. Others might be mediocre at both and need help identifying their strengths and what makes them unique.

The good news is that you can help your child develop a healthy self-image and help them feel secure about themselves.

1. Model positive self-image.

2. Listen to what your child says when they talk about their self-image and validate your child's feelings.

3. Praise your child for their characteristics, their positive qualities, and the positive choices they make.

4. Explain the impact that social media and peers have on one's self-image.

5. Let your child know that what they are feeling is normal. Talk to your child about whether they set unrealistic expectations for themselves, which sets them up for failure.

Celebrate Individuality and Personal Strengths

Fitting in is important to many tweens. They want to have friends and be socially accepted. They are afraid to let their individuality shine. It can be scary if they are perceived to be different. However, parents can help their children embrace their individuality. Below are proven methods that you can apply.

1. Ask your child what activities they want to be involved in and respect their preferences. You might want them to join football or soccer, but they really want to be in the drama club. Please give them the freedom to make their own choices.

2. Give your child the freedom to choose their wardrobe (within reason). Every person has their style, and their clothes can positively express who they are.

3. Although it might be difficult, let your child have control over their body, within reason. If they want to try purple hair, if it's safe and not permanent, allow them to experiment on weekends outside the school campus.

4. Give your child a safe place to express how they feel. Listen to what they say without judgment, even if you think it's silly.

5. Accept and love your children for who they are.

6. Please encourage your child to think about what they do well. Give positive, constructive feedback as your child works to develop their strengths and overcome their weaknesses. Encourage your child to use a growth mindset and seek help to overcome perceived weakness. Set reasonable expectations for your child, and then celebrate when they meet or exceed those expectations.

7. Praise your child for their effort in accomplishing a task instead of the end result. Every day, talk with your child about something they excelled

at and praise their effort.

8. Share positive affirmations with your child. Affirmations can be as simple as I am beautiful, I am smart, I am confident, I love myself, etc. Ask your child to write affirmations in a journal or on a sticky, and place the written affirmations in visible places such as desks or walls.

Key Takeaways

- Please encourage your child to be independent while setting reasonable expectations for them.

- Speak with your child about being responsible and how they can be accountable, whether doing their chores or making good decisions.

- Help your child make good decisions. Don't get angry if they make a bad decision. Talk about the situation with your child and what they can do differently next time.

- Listen, with empathy, when your child talks about their self-image or self-esteem. Please encourage them to think about their positive qualities.

- Give your child the freedom to be who they feel they are and to explore their individuality within reason.

- Celebrate your child's strengths while encouraging them to strengthen their weaker areas.

- Try to model positive self-esteem and positive self-image.

In this chapter, we learned how to help your child boost confidence and encourage them to identify their strengths. When children become more independent within boundaries and feel confident about themselves without being cocky, your parenting job will be easier because you no longer have to feel the need or go out of your way to create a bubble to protect your child. Life is full of ups and downs, even for independent and confident people. The next chapter will discuss how to help your child develop resilience and flexibility when things don't turn out as expected.

CHAPTER 4: BUILD RESILIENCE AND FLEXIBILITY

"Success is not final. Failure is not fatal. It is the courage to continue that counts."

— *Winston Churchill*

We have learned the art of instilling freedom into our tweens attending middle schools; now, it is time to help them learn from their mistakes. From a very young age, we have learned that when you fall off a bike, you brush off the dirt, get back on, and try again. This is called resilience, the 'never giving up' mentality or attitude. Raising resilient children empowers them to tackle different and challenging situations in middle school and beyond.

Resilience and flexibility go hand in hand. Flexibility, which supports the development of resilience, is thinking about situations, people, etc., in different scenarios and with different perspectives. A flexible mindset lets children handle disappointments, challenges, and successes in healthy ways. It also helps children come up with creative solutions to problems. Encountering challenges is part of life; the key is not to be defeated by them while trying to be resilient and flexible. You can help your child successfully navigate life challenges and make parenting easier for you once your child develops resilience and an adaptable mindset.

Navigate Change and Uncertainty

Lynn Lyons, a licensed social worker and psychotherapist, states, "We have become a culture of trying to ensure our children are comfortable. We as parents are trying to stay one step ahead of everything our tweens and teenagers will encounter. The problem? Life doesn't work that way." Lyons also says that our job, as parents, is to help children handle uncertainty and solve problems. And that's how they learn to be resilient. Below are key methods through which you can help your children become more resilient:

1. Don't accommodate all of your child's requests. For example, if they ask for wishes that cannot be fulfilled, help them understand with a loving talk. If it's simply outside your budget to pay for two Taylor Swift concert tickets, explain money management basics instead of dismissing your daughter's request and explain prioritizing needs over wants.

2. Let them experience controlled risks to learn about dangers in the world and how to deal with them.

3. Teach your child problem-solving skills. Whenever you are with your children, casually mention some problems and then ask for solutions, such as how they can solve them.

4. When your child makes a mistake, ask how they will fix it instead of why it happened.

5. Please don't give your child all the answers; instead, let them address questions and doubts independently. If they ask questions like "What happens if we do this? Or what happens if we do that?" instead of telling them everything immediately, let them delve into it and figure it out independently. When riding a bicycle, they might ask, "What if we peddle too fast?" You can ask them, "Why don't you try it?" What will happen? You can catch your child from the back when they are about to fall. You let your child explore and learn while being there for them.

6. Encourage and model resilience as much as you can. Allow them to do things independently and experience mistakes and failures within reason. For example, encourage them to try out for school sports teams, and they might get rejected. Tell your children rejection is part of life; what is important is getting back up and trying again. Ask them to do some yard work or cook in the kitchen. They will make some mistakes. As long as they learn from their mistakes and continue, you are helping them build resilience.

Guide Your Child to Adapt to New Environments and Expectations

When your child first enters middle school, it is a new environment where teachers have higher expectations than their elementary school teachers. You can guide your child to adapt to new environments earlier, which will make parenting easier for you soon.

1. Get your child's school schedule ahead of time and find each class in order.

2. When your child starts middle school, you can walk with them to find their locker, the bathrooms, the cafeteria, and the office on orientation day. Ask your child to think about how much time they have between classes, plan their optimal routes to classrooms that are farther apart, etc.

3. Review the student handbook with your child to ensure your child knows the rules and policies.

4. If possible, attend every open house and parent-teacher conference to understand each teacher's expectations, which can vary from one teacher to another, and explain those to your child.

5. Please encourage your child to advocate for themselves. When they need help understanding what's being taught in a class, ask them to follow up with the teacher for clarification; don't wait until low test results come back to ask for help.

6. Neither you nor your child should overreact to a bad grade at first. It takes time for your child to get used to the middle school grading system and teachers' expectations. As long as your child realizes where and how they can improve, every bad grade is a learning opportunity to do better next time.

7. Please encourage your child to socialize with peers, whether playing sports or watching movies. Some children have this preconceived notion that they must be friends first to socialize. Let them know peers they socialize with may not turn into friends but can be study partners and lunch buddies. Your child's friends may not have much time to socialize with them because middle schoolers can get pretty busy, and their friends may want to mingle with new people. We will discuss this topic more in Chapter 7 - Social Skills and Relationships.

Embrace Change with a Flexible Mindset

Your child will encounter many changes during middle school, some bigger than others. Treating each change with an open mind and flexible approaches can help your child survive and thrive during changes.

You can use the following proven methods to help your child become more flexible and handle life's changes.

1. Validate your child's emotions when they resist changes.

2. Please encourage them to come up with solutions.

3. Practice flexibility, which can be as simple as getting alternative food choices. For example, suppose your family's favorite pizzeria runs out of pepperoni pizza. In that case, you ask your child whether he'd like to have plain cheese or sausage pizza. Then, praise your child for being flexible.

4. Teach your child to talk themselves through a problem or situation when stuck. Please encourage them to say things out loud and think about alternative solutions.

5. Ask your child to keep an open mind; don't assume the worst case when things and circumstances change.

Guide Your Child to Cultivate a Growth Mindset

A growth mindset means your child fully believes they can continue learning and growing. Let your child know that one's intelligence and capabilities can be developed and increased through learning, successes and failures, and conscious training. Your child will believe they can accomplish their goals if they continue to work toward them despite setbacks. Guiding your child to cultivate a growth mindset also makes your parenting job much easier because your child is more open to changes and more motivated to learn new things without you trying to push them. A growth mindset is essential for many reasons.

1. Children with a growth mindset are more motivated.

2. They are more resilient.

3. They don't take failures personally. Instead, they learn from their mistakes and keep trying.

4. They understand that challenges are a part of life.

5. They take pleasure in learning.

6. Children with a growth mindset achieve more and are more successful.

Here's how you can help your child develop a growth mindset:

1. Praise your child's effort; don't just focus on the end result. Instead of saying, "I'm so proud that you got an A" when they ace a test, tell them,

"You studied hard for this exam. I'm proud of your effort, which paid off." That way, your child's motivation and sense of achievement are not limited to that one letter grade; they know you're proud of their effort.

2. Show your child that failing isn't a bad thing. Let them know one bad grade doesn't define their ability. Gently ask them, "What did you learn from this exam?" "How do you plan to improve?" "Where do you think you need help?"

3. Encourage your child to love learning. Ask them what interests them and help them learn more about it. Help them understand that learning is a lifelong journey that is fun and rewarding. Learning is about more than just getting good grades. Learning includes self-discovery.

4. Model a growth mindset. Don't dwell on mistakes; learn from them and move forward. Tell your child about a time you made a mistake, what you learned from it, and how you improved because of what you learned.

Overcoming Challenges and Setbacks

Michael Jordan is one of the best examples of how resilience leads to success. He said, "I've missed more than 9,000 shots in my career. I've lost almost 300 games. Twenty-six times, I've been trusted to take the game-winning shot and missed. I've failed over and over again in my life. And that's why I succeed."

Problem-solving skills are necessary for overcoming challenges and setbacks. You can help your child develop these skills.

1. Identify the problem. Ask your child to tell you the problem so you can see the situation from their perspective. Then, discuss how to solve the problem.

2. Discuss why the issue is a problem and what is causing it.

3. Brainstorm at least three solutions to the problem and what the consequences could be.

4. Analyze the pros and cons of each solution.

5. Once your child has decided which solution would be best, encourage them to act on it.

6. After the solution has been put into play, talk about what happened. What went well and what didn't?

Foster Persistence and Positive Thinking

Henry Ford said, "If you think you can or you think you can't, you're right." It is the true power of positive thinking, which is incredible. It tells you the difference between success and failure. Positive thinking is crucial to persistence, resilience, and a growth mindset. You can help your child develop positive thinking through the following.

1. Ask your child to tell you three things that went well every day. Then, share three things that went well in your day.

2. Once a day, talk about what you and your child are grateful for. They can also thank someone who did something nice for them.

3. Please encourage your child to discuss an overwhelming or stressful situation and how they worked through it. Help your child identify what triggers negative thoughts. Assure them that they can get through the problem.

4. Again, praise your child for their effort to accomplish tasks, not the result as discussed above.

5. Explain to your child what negative self-talk is. Tell them that negativity snowballs, and others will pop up once they start believing one negative thought.

6. Encourage positive self-talk, regardless of setbacks. Teach your child to replace negative thoughts with positive ones or take a break. When your child starts to have negative thoughts, please encourage them to go for a walk, ride their bike, or do other physical activities. It increases dopamine and other feel-good chemicals in the brain.

7. Avoid comparing your child to others. No two people are alike, and it's unfair to expect them to be.

Key Takeaways

- Guild your child to be resilient. Let your child know that challenges and failures are sometimes the best part of life because failures can breed success in the long run. Remind your child that some of the most successful people in the world failed at first.

- Explain to your child that changes are a part of life that happens often. Help them become flexible and adapt to changes by changing their routines or making new game rules.

- Please help your child navigate their middle school life by allowing them to have new experiences while letting them know you are in their corner.

- Teach your child that the key to success is knowing they can achieve their goals and being persistent. Help them practice positive thinking every day.

While you are helping your child build resilience and develop a flexible mindset, stress can pop up for both your child. Next, let's discuss how to foster stress management in your child, which also helps reduce stress for you as a parent.

CHAPTER 5: STRESS MANAGEMENT AND SELF-CARE

"It's not stress that kills us; it is our reaction to it."

– Hans Selye

We are living in a fast-moving world where your tweens are facing information overload, high academic, peer, and social pressure, and complex relationship dynamics. Helping your child manage stress and encourage them to prioritize mental self-care is essential to developing resilience and self-confidence. Sometimes, a healthy dosage of pressure can be good, as it can help us get things done on time. An example of healthy pressure is that your child knows they have to finish a project for science class, and they plan to get it done right and on time. It becomes stressful to them and you when they don't make a plan and desperately try to complete the project the day before it is due.

Pressure can create anxiety, which can have a lasting effect on your child's mental health. It starts to affect one's mental and physical health. And if your child doesn't have an outlet, a support system, or even good coping skills, it can get more triggering. It can also become an alarming situation if there is no break from the constant cycle of stress. Therefore, establishing healthy routines and self-care can help you and your child manage stress.

Cope with Stress and Anxiety

Your child may experience different types of stress, some come from within and some are caused by external factors. Some types of stress can be transient, while other types of stress can be ongoing to severe. For example:

- One is a reaction to challenges, changes, or time constraints, such as getting projects done on time or not having friends during the 1st week of middle school.

- Self-imposed stress for 1) Overly ambitious children or children who tend to be perfectionists. And 2). Children with low self-esteem who worry about how peers view them.

- Chronic stress is when life makes you and your child stressed for over a few weeks. This type of stress can cause severe mental and physical health conditions, such as depression, anxiety, insomnia, high blood pressure, and others.

- Traumatic stress happens when a serious event occurs, such as a major injury, violence, or a severe accident. When your child is stressed out, so are you.

Identify Stressors and Anxiety Triggers

Although stress is a normal part of life, certain events or situations often cause your child to be even more stressed out and anxious. By understanding these triggers, you can help your child cope with their stress and anxiety. Please speak with your child when you sense they are anxious and stressed. Ask them what specific event or situation caused it.

- Keep a journal. Each time your child is stressed and/or anxious, write down everything about the situation that you can think of, including the time of day, who is around, what happened just before, and even what they ate before the anxiety started.

- Ask them to tell you about anything that is going on in their life that they can't stop thinking about, such as a situation at school, an issue with a friend, or something at home.

- Actively listen to your child without judgment about what is happening in their life. Let your child know you will not judge them or anything they tell you so they are willing to share their triggers with you.

- Let them open up to you, which can happen when you validate their feelings. It will make them feel seen and even heard.

Practical Techniques for Stress Reduction

There is no instant cure for stress; it doesn't simply go away overnight. However, you can help alleviate your child's stress and help them healthily handle life's curveballs. While you are at it, practice some of these tips to help you deal with your own stress.

1. Ask your child to share their schedule with you, including everything from upcoming projects, assignments, and activities with friends. Then, help them create a plan for everything, mapping out ways to accomplish those. This hands-on approach works well for children struggling with the increased workload in middle school or still trying to adjust to new environments. Initial handholding is necessary while cultivating their self-confidence and flexibility and showing that you are there for your child every step of their middle school journey.

2. Help your child brainstorm solutions for the difficult situations that are causing them stress. This approach works well if your child has a strong personality and wants independence, because you are not giving answers but empowering them to cope with challenges, while having their back.

3. Provide routines for your child, such as getting up and going to bed at the same time and eating meals together. Doing things systematically and according to routine also helps with stress management greatly.

4. Get your child a notebook or journal so they can write about their life's events. Journaling is a great way to express one's emotions while feeling safe and private.

5. If your child isn't into writing, buy a sketchbook or coloring book and some colored pencils, gel pens, markers, or paints to relieve stress. As we discussed in Chapter 1, coloring books or artistic expressions are a great way to channel emotions and they work equally well for children.

6. Teach or provide resources to help your child practice meditation, yoga, or breathing techniques to proactively prevent and relieve stress. We also discussed this for you to practice in Chapter 1. Now you can transfer these mental and emotional self-care skills to your child, win-win!

7. Encourage your child to exercise regularly. You can take bristle walks, jog, bike, or play sports together. It not only releases stress, but increases feel-good hormones, such as serotonin and dopamine, which improves mood and reduces cortisol.

8. Interact with nature as it also helps manage and reduce stress. Be it plant-

ing a flower, taking a hike, or simply going outdoors and enjoying the trees, listening to the sounds of the birds, and the scurrying of squirrels, any of these acts can help greatly.

9. Please encourage your child to take a break from whatever they are doing. Sticking to one thing for a long time too can cause stress so they take a break and play a game, hang out with their friends, listen to music, read a book, or just do something as they please.

10. If outside forces, such as bullying, cause stress, be your child's advocate and help them address the situation. Let them know that you will always be there for them.

11. Give your child opportunities to use their strengths to neutralize or overcome their insecurity and anxiety. If they are good at singing, encourage them to join music groups at school. Encourage them to join the drama club if they are funny or good at acting. Also, encourage them to leverage their strengths and follow their passion to do productive things (e.g., playing games all day doesn't count), even if their passions don't align with your interests.

12. Give your child choices and a say in potential plans when it is possible and reasonable to help them feel they have some control of their life.

13. Let your child know how you deal with your own stress, such as by doing deep breathing exercises, talking to a friend, journaling, or doing some form of physical exercise.

Importance of Cultivating Self-Care for Middle Schoolers

Self-care is essential for both your child and for yourself. As discussed in Chapter 1, you can only be the person and parent you want to be if you are taking care of yourself. On top of that, the easiest way to teach your child how to take care of themselves is to model it. There are other benefits of self-care as well.

1. Your child will be able to identify what they need, physically and emotionally. They will know how to take care of those needs.

2. Self-care will teach your child responsibility.

3. Good self-care habits will help reduce stress, anxiety, and other mental health disorders.

4. Your child will be more energetic and ready to tackle challenges and

tasks.

5. Self-care reduces the chances of becoming sick.

6. Learning self-care techniques can foster resilience.

Establish Healthy Routines

Help your child learn to practice self-care by establishing healthy routines, which sound familiar, right? Well, many strategies and tips we discussed in Chapter 1 about how you can stay healthy and energetic also apply to your child. Remember, you have always been a teacher to your child, whether you realize it or not. At this age, your child still models after you. When you and your child practice healthy living together, it becomes a family routine, which makes your parenting job easier.

1. Talk about good sleep hygiene to ensure they (and you) get enough rest.

2. Go to bed at the same time every night.

3. Get up at the same time every morning.

4. Keep the room dark and cool.

5. Avoid using electronics with blue screens at least a half hour before bed.

6. Don't drink any caffeine for a couple of hours before bed.

7. Exercise routinely, but not right before bed.

8. Learn mindful relaxation methods such as meditation, yoga, deep breathing, and positive visualization techniques with your child.

9. Eat balanced meals and healthy snacks. Don't let your child binge eat sweets and starchy foods when they feel stressed. That instant gratification will cause their blood sugar to crash soon after eating, making them lethargic. Eat fruits instead to give a mood boost without added sugar. Let your child take part in planning the meals and shopping for the ingredients. Then, prepare the meals together.

10. Develop a regular exercise routine that you and your child do together for at least thirty minutes each day. This can be as simple as going for a walk, going to the gym, or taking a yoga class together.

11. Create routines, such as morning routines for getting ready for school, homework, eating, showering, downtime, and bedtime.

Key Takeaways

- Remember that stress and anxiety are a part of life; the key is to manage stress and prevent anxiety as much as possible proactively.

- Please help your child identify what triggers their stress and anxiety. Then, work with them to develop coping mechanisms when they are triggered.

- Please work with your child to help them learn essential techniques to reduce stress.

- Establish healthy routines for your child so they know how to practice self-care.

- Practice self-care with your child together, and be a role model for your child.

Since this chapter focuses on stress handling and management, let's take a deep breath. Next, let's learn how to help your child develop emotional intelligence.

PART 3. CULTIVATE YOUR CHILD'S EMOTIONAL INTELLIGENCE, COMMUNICATION, AND SOCIAL SKILLS

CHAPTER 6: EMOTIONAL INTELLIGENCE

"It is very important to understand that emotional intelligence is not the opposite of intelligence, it is not the triumph of heart over head – it is the unique intersection of both."

– David Caruso

The previous chapter discussed that stress can be self-imposed or caused by external factors. Understanding and introducing emotional intelligence is also integral to helping your child thrive in life and prevent and reduce stress stemming from the inner self and external factors.

What exactly is Emotional Intelligence (EI)? There might be different interpretations of EI. I will keep the definition simple and concise. EI is the ability to manage our own emotions and understand the emotions of others around us. There are five key elements of EI:

- Self-awareness

- Self-regulation

- Empathy

- Social skills

- Motivation

We will spread EI development across multiple chapters because EI is often coupled with other essential skills. This chapter will focus on methods to help your child develop self-awareness, self-regulation, and empathy.

Research has shown that children whose parents have lower emotional intelligence might struggle to manage their own emotions since they have less opportunity to learn healthy coping skills. Therefore, as parents, we need to remind ourselves that our children model after us; we need to regulate our emotions and be perceptive, understanding, and empathetic when our children get emotional.

These are key benefits to help your child develop emotional intelligence.

1. Children with higher levels of emotional intelligence tend to be more successful.

2. Emotional intelligence also helps children form stronger relationships with others and learn to handle conflicts better.

3. Studies have shown that tweens who have developed emotional intelligence are more successful as adults.

4. There is a link between higher levels of emotional intelligence and a decrease in mental illnesses, such as depression.

We are not born with emotional intelligence, an acquired capability that can be developed at any age. As your child's first and most influential teacher, you can help your child grow and acquire these skills. You might wonder, "I'm hot-tempered already; how do I teach my child to develop EI?" Don't worry; I will break it down into manageable and actionable steps for you.

The best music instrument teachers or sports coaches don't have to be the best performers in their respective fields. They are wise about whom they coach and know how to apply the right coaching techniques to individual players. No one knows your child better than you, right?

Encourage Self-Awareness

Consider the following scenario:

"I hate school. I hate the teacher and everyone else," your son Sam said, slamming his backpack on the floor.

"How come?" you asked.

"They're dumb," he replied.

Right then, you want to figure out how to get to the root of Sam's anger and frustration.

"Let me get you a snack. We'll talk."

You put Sam's favorite snack on the table and asked, "Which class and which teacher upset you."

"English class. Mrs. Bennett." He snapped.

"What happened?" You gently asked.

"She made us write a paragraph using figurative language. I couldn't think of anything to write. I got metaphors and similes confused," Sam sounded angry.

Now you know the cause of Sam's frustration. Next is to get him to name his feelings.

"How did you feel when you were confused?" You whispered, not to dial his anger more, but to assist him in realizing that you are there, listening and showing interest in what he feels

"I was mad, and I felt dumb because everyone else knew the difference." He said, his flushed cheeks showing his frustration loud and clear.

At that point, through a couple of open-ended questions, you were able to get Sam to not only explain what the problem is but also name his emotions. You validated his emotions. The next step is to tell Same that you will help him work on the assignment and learn the difference between a metaphor and a simile.

Help Your Child Self-Regulate through Identifying and Expressing Emotions

Slamming doors, stomping feet, and yelling are indications that someone is having a bad day. Everyone experiences them. The easiest way to handle these emotions is to give the feelings a name and then learn how to express them in a healthy way. This can be challenging as an adult. It is even more so for an adolescent. That's where you can help them.

Talk to your child about how they are feeling. Please help them name their emotions, as shown in the example above, whether they are anger, frustration, sadness, etc. Once your kid labels their feelings and realizes that you understand them, they will feel relieved.

First, ask open-ended questions such as:

1. How are you feeling? If they say I don't know, then give examples. Are you angry? Are you frustrated? Are you sad?

2. Why are you feeling this way?

3. What happened to make you feel this way? Talking about it will make you feel better.

Next, be open with your child about your frustrations as an example and explain why talking about them is healthy. They know when you are angry, happy, sad, etc. Talk to them about how you are feeling and why you are feeling this way, i.e., the source of those emotions, like where they are stemming from. This not only models the skills you are trying to teach, but it will also help them understand how your emotions affect them.

"I'm frustrated. A lot of little things happened today, like spilling my coffee, being late to a meeting, and dropping my sandwich at lunch because I was worried about how my boss felt about being late to an important meeting. Thanks to you, I feel better now that I've told you how I feel and why." See, it can be this easy; you just need to take the first step, and the magic will happen, starting from there. This might make you feel a bit vulnerable, sharing your mistakes with your child because you are supposed to be this super dad or mom in front of your child. Trust me, it will strengthen your bond with your child when you open up more with your child. You and your child might laugh after hearing your silly mistakes that frustrated you.

Then, help your child understand that it is perfectly normal to have different moods at home. For example, you might be grumpy when you first wake up in the morning or feel stressed when trying to take care of everything that needs to be done before rushing out the door. Talk to them about how your mood affects other people and vice versa.

"This morning, I was grouchy because I was thinking about everything I had to get done today. I snapped at you, and it made you grouchy, too." Another example is, "Remember when I started laughing last night while we were playing the game, and you started laughing too? Everyone in the house was having fun." It is simple and easy. You just need to bridge the gaps and deal with it smoothly.

Talking to your child openly and honestly about your feelings can help them understand their feelings and how they affect others. It can also help them realize that their feelings are valid and that they are entitled to them.

Alternative Ways to Encourage Your Child to Express Emotions

We all know that sometimes, talking about feelings has its limitations and sometimes doesn't work when your child doesn't want to talk about anything and wants to be left alone. There are other ways that you can help your adolescents express themselves. As discussed in previous sections about coping with stress and mental self-care, let's review these proven methods.

1. Please encourage your child to use a journal and write down their emotions. Buy them a diary, journal, notebook, and a pen they like. Promise them you won't read what they write unless they ask you to.

2. Maybe your adolescent doesn't like to write. Please encourage them to use a sketchbook or coloring book to channel their emotions. Later, when they feel like it, they offer to talk about their work, what they created, and why they made it.

3. Go for a walk, whether it is a walk around the block, in the park, or a hike. Ask your child how their day was and name one exciting thing that happened. Let the conversation flow from there.

4. Ask your child to find a song that expresses how they feel. If they look at you as though you've grown a second head, then put on a song that describes your thoughts and feelings and explain why.

5. Do something that you both enjoy. This can be as simple as watching a sports game, grocery shopping, or even taking a bike ride together. Sometimes, even playing games together also helps. These might seem like simple and small activities, but they let your child know that you are there for them and experience their emotions with them.

6. You know your child better than anyone else. Engage them in an activity that relaxes them and gets them talking. Be ready to listen and empathize. Validate their feelings.

7. I can see why you would feel that way.

8. That situation would frustrate me, too.

Help Your Child Develop Empathy

Empathy means that you can understand what other people are thinking and feeling. Empathy is different from sympathy, which means you feel sorry for someone. While empathizing with someone, you can understand and share another person's feelings. For example, when your child feels a particular emotion, after scoring less than expected on a test, you don't scold them but instead understand their emotions by putting yourself in their shoes. You want to help your child develop empathy to better interact with peers and teachers in middle school and beyond.

There are a lot of benefits to helping your child develop empathy.

- Your child may become more self-aware.

- Empathy will help them understand other people's needs and feelings.

- Your child will be able to form more meaningful friendships and other relationships.

- They will be able to communicate more effectively.

- Empathy decreases bullying.

- Your child will have an increased tolerance and acceptance of others - even those different from them.

- They will become more successful as an adult.

There are several methods that you can use to help your child become more empathetic.

1. As always, be a role model. First, when you communicate with your child, give them your full attention. Ask questions and talk to them about how they feel. Please encourage them to tell you why they are having those feelings.

2. You can also display this in your everyday life. Let's learn it through an example. Let's say you are at a grocery store, and the cashier is grouchy. They are slamming your items down on the conveyor belt and tossing them in the bags. At this point, you have a choice. You can yell at the cashier about their attitude or empathize. Ask how their day is and mention that you know their job can be challenging. Some people don't appreciate how tough their job is. The cashier might not change how they act, but your child will see how you handled the situation. Afterward, you can say, "I feel bad for them. They must be having a rough day."

3. Ask your child to see the situation from another person's perspective. "I know you are frustrated because your friend wanted to hang out with someone else today. Why do you think they wanted to?" If you get the standard shoulder shrug and "I don't know stare," provide some scenarios. "They sit with you every day. They still like and care about you, but they want to be friends with someone else, too."

4. History has many teachable moments. Point out events that happened in the past and how other people showed empathy. For example, you can discuss Irene Sendler and how she saved over 2,500 Jewish children. Such real-life examples and references help in ways you can not even imagine.

5. Ask your child to think about someone at school who might be the target of bullying or may not have friends. Encourage them to talk about how that person feels and how your child might feel if they were in the other person's shoes—even telling them to be friends with that kid and trying to be there for them.

6. Praise your child when showing empathy toward another person. "That's very kind of you." "I'm proud of you for being so thoughtful." Telling them how proud you are will motivate them to do more and more the next time. Getting rewarded, either with words or even actions, can be a great agent of encouragement.

The different elements of EI go hand in hand. When your child develops empathy, you will notice that they become more self-motivated to help you with house chores and volunteer at community centers. Your child will be able to relate to others better, understand their teachers' and peers' perspectives, and self-regulate their frustrations toward teachers and peers.

Key Takeaways

- Emotional intelligence is an acquired capability that consists of self-awareness, self-regulation, empathy, social skills, and motivation.

- Please help your child increase self-awareness by asking open-ended questions without judgment and leading them to discuss their feelings.

- It helps your child self-regulate their emotions by identifying and expressing their feelings.

- Apply verbal and non-verbal methods to help your child channel their emotions.

- Help your child develop empathy for others, which in turn can help your child self-regulate and develop healthy relationships with others.

Now that you have learned methods to cultivate three critical elements of EI in your child, let's discuss how to help your child communicate effectively, which also puts the EI they acquired into practice.

Chapter 7: Effective Communication

"Nothing in life is more important than the ability to communicate effectively."

– Gerald R. Ford, former United States president

Words are powerful. Often, what we communicate to each other directly affects the relationships we have with others and the outcome of a conversation. When transitioning from elementary school to middle school, your tweens not only start using more complex vocabulary and sentences but also need to be more aware of how they communicate with others, which can impact relationships, trigger emotional responses, and impact conversation outcomes. Communication skills and emotional intelligence go hand-in-hand. Emotional intelligence directly contributes to effective communication. Effective communication can also help with social skills, an important element of EI that I will discuss in Chapter 8.

Cultivate Effective Communication Skills

Many people think that effective communication means that both parties get to talk and express their opinions. However, there is much more to effective communication. Emotional intelligence plays a critical role in effective communication. The choice of words and tone we use can make a big difference in the communication outcome and quality of our relationships with others. Key benefits of effective communication skills include:

- Forming meaningful relationships with other people. Your child will be able to explain what they need from the relationship and will understand other people's needs.

- Reducing conflicts and helping with conflict resolution.

- Self-advocating and asking for what they need and want.

- Being able to read and interpret nonverbal cues.

- Being more successful academically, as well as in life down the road.

Like other skills, you can teach your child how to communicate effectively. You might hesitate, "Wait, I'm not a great communicator. How can I teach my child to communicate effectively?" That's the beauty of teaching. We often become better in a field once we start teaching others in the same field. Take a deep breath. Let's go over these steps, which are easier than you think. Again, if your child can communicate effectively with you at home and with others outside the home, your parenting job will be much easier.

1. Demonstrate active listening and effective communication. Put away any distractions. Focus on what your child is trying to tell you. If you don't understand, ask clarifying questions, which helps your child raise awareness of how they communicate.

2. Show your child how to respond to angry outbursts calmly. Keep your voice low and even, although you might feel anxious and boiling inside. Monitor your body language and keep your composure. For example, you don't raise your voice when your child has an angry outburst. Instead, you keep your voice gentle and calm.

3. Encourage your child to ask for clarification if they don't understand what someone is trying to say. "I'm sorry, I didn't understand what you meant. Could you please explain it to me?"

4. Practice conversations with your child to prepare them for social events. School dances, PTA parties, and other social events will start popping up more and more. For some tweens, these events can be nerve-racking for some shy children. Tell them how they can break ice with peers at social events.

5. Watch a movie with your child or read the same book and initiate a conversation about it. Ask what they liked and didn't like and why. Ask questions like "Was there something in the movie you didn't understand? Also, ask your middle schoolers their opinion about a movie, a book, an actor, or anything they might find interesting. Ask questions about their views. Then, tell your child your opinion so they can ask you questions.

6. Doing a home, school, or playful project together is a great way to promote effective communication and teamwork. Both of you have to listen to the other's ideas and communicate your thoughts. For example, you can do a fun project with just a bag of balloons and a roll of masking tape. Your goal, working together, is to build the tallest freestanding structure that you can -- without talking or communicating in any way. Then, do the same project again, only this time, you both share your ideas. Talk about the different experiences. Which project was more successful? Which project was more frustrating?

7. Role-playing is another great way to develop communication skills. Pull a scene out of a hat, like two friends trying to decide what they want to do for the weekend, two friends having an argument, or talking to a teacher about something the student didn't understand. Practice having the conversation. Then, switch roles so your child can experience what being in the other person's shoes is like.

8. Teach your child how to respond respectfully. Instead of telling a person, "You're wrong," they can say, "I disagree, or I'm not sure I agree with you. This is why."

Nonverbal Communication

Actions speak louder than words is a true statement, in more ways than one. Nonverbal communication is often more powerful than verbal communication. Think about this: Have you ever heard someone say "Good morning" but their tone tells you that they do not wish you a good morning? Tone is only one example of nonverbal communication. Other examples include:

- Facial expressions — eye-rolling, frowns, smiles, lips pressed together, etc.

- Posture — arms crossed and leaning back in a chair indicate that the person is not listening. On the flip side, leaning forward with open arms tells the talker that the listener is ready to listen and understand what the other person is saying. Rocking back and forth or fidgeting with hands indicates that the person is nervous. Posture can send out other messages as well. A person who walks with their head up, their back straight, looks people in the eye, and speaks in a clear, audible tone portrays confidence. A person who is slumped over, eyes on the ground, and isn't easily heard signals that they lack self-confidence.

- Gestures — I don't mean a particular gesture that some people are fond of giving, which does communicate a clear message. For example, flailing your arms can signify anger or excitement.

- Eye contact and movement — In the United States and some other countries, maintaining eye contact when communicating is considered respectful. Looking up and to the side usually means that the person is trying to remember something or figure out what they will say. Keep in mind in some cultures, such as Japan and Korea, maintaining direct eye contact is considered disrespectful. Therefore, let your child know to be mindful about different cultural customs when your family travels to other countries for vacation.

Explain to your child the different types of nonverbal communication. Practice each of them. Not only will it get some laughs, but it will demonstrate the power of nonverbal communication. Discuss the fact that spoken words can be negated by nonverbal communication. "I love you," followed by an eye roll, is a sure sign that the statement is not genuine.

An effective way to teach the power of nonverbal skills is to watch people. Go to the mall or the park. Ask your child to pay attention to facial expressions, gestures, tone of voice, and other non-verbal cues. Take turns quietly discussing your perception of those people's gestures, tones, etc.

You can also practice with your child when watching your favorite television show. Turn off the volume and watch the actors' nonverbal communication. Then ask your child what they think the actors in the show are feeling. Rewatch the same segment with volume and have the same discussion. Did the actors' nonverbal communication match what they said?

Active Listening

There is a difference between hearing and listening. Hearing means that your eardrums have captured the vibrations in the air and have processed the fact that there was some sound. Listening means that you know and understand what is being said. Getting your child to slow down long enough to listen to anything might be a miracle, but once you have their attention, there are ways to help them learn important active listening skills.

- Model active listening. When your child is talking, ensure they have your undivided attention. Ask related questions to let them know that you are listening.

- Please remind your child to put away distractions such as their devices.

- Practice paraphrasing: "You are angry because you didn't understand the assignment because..." This way, your child will feel that you pay attention to what they tell you.

- Role-play the opposite of active listening. Tell your child ahead of time what you are going to do, and then have them tell you a story about something that happened to them. Then, interrupt them and then start talking about something else. Don't give them a chance to speak. Afterwards, ask them how that felt and how the conversation could have improved.

- Demonstrate nonverbal cues of active listening. Lean towards them with your arms open. Keep eye contact. Verbally let your child know that you are listening by saying things such as yes, I see, uh-huh, and nod when appropriate.

- To take active listening to another level, you can discuss a topic your child may not understand. Encourage them to ask questions to clarify information, even if the topic does not immediately grab their attention. Ask them to discuss a topic that you may need to learn a lot, such as their multi-role game. And you demonstrate asking questions to clarify details.

Constructive Feedback

Feedback is a reaction to something that another person has done or said. It can be constructive or destructive. Your child needs to understand that 1). When they receive less positive feedback, they should treat it as a learning or reflection moment. 2) When they give less positive feedback to others, it doesn't have to be harsh or mean.

Teach them phrases such as "I think you may have made a mistake" instead of "Why did you do something so silly?" or "You made a mistake." Words like "I think" and "may" can make a big difference on the receiving end. These words give a softer and more compassionate tone. Help them learn that constructive feedback should be given immediately. It should be honest, gentle, supportive, and specific. For example, you can model giving constructive feedback: "You did a good job cleaning your room today, and it would be great if you could help clean up the living room where you left your clothes around."

Conflict Resolution

Your child is at an age where conflicts are natural. They have conflicts with their classmates, siblings, teachers, you, and anyone else who looks at them differently or from a different perspective. The key is learning how to de-escalate, neutralize a situation, and resolve the conflict. Demonstrate how to use "I" statements. Explain to your child that "I" statements will make the other person feel less defensive and more willing to discuss the situation.

Encourage problem-solving skills. Ask them to think of different solutions to the problems and the consequences of each option. When you disagree with your child, ask them to sit down with you. State the issue that you are having. Then, brainstorm ways that the problem can be solved. Ask your child to consider potential solutions.

- Teach your child about compromise and win-win. Describe a situation when you had to compromise with another person. Ask them to describe a situation when a compromise would have solved a problem. Ask them to think about the other person's point of view and come up with solutions that would solve everyone's problem. For example, your child and their friends argued about what to do or eat during a playdate. Teach your child about taking turns when debating with their friends about whether to play soccer or watch a movie, having pizza or sandwiches for lunch.

- Please remind your child that people, children, and adults sometimes lose their tempers during conflict. Give them some tips, such as breathing deeply, counting to ten, or taking a break from the problem and returning to it when they have calmed down.

Assertive Communication

Being assertive is a lot different from being aggressive. Being assertive means standing up for yourself in a respectful yet firm manner. It means advocating for yourself, asking for help, or asking what you need. Here the benefits of assertive communication:

- It is empowering and gives the child control over the situation they're dealing with.

- Saying no allows your child to set healthy boundaries for themselves.

- Your child will be less overwhelmed by saying no to something they really don't want to do.

- Your child will be less likely to give in to peer pressure.

- They tend to have higher self-esteem.

Assertive communication can be difficult for adults. It might be even more challenging for middle schoolers trying to fit in. Yet you can teach them how to be assertive, which will help them now and as adults.

- Discuss the difference between **passive, aggressive, and assertive communication**.

- Passive communication is giving in or hiding from the issue. For example: "I guess so if you want to."

- Aggressive is attacking, such as "You always get me in trouble when we go to the bowling alley."

- Assertive is calm and direct communication. For example, "I don't want to go to the party tomorrow night. I have to study because my grades are important."

- Help your child understand boundaries. Those are lines that should not be crossed. Tell your child about some of your boundaries, and be clear and stern about them, stating the consequence of crossing them. Remind them that they should also set boundaries, such as not letting people touch or hug them without asking for permission first or not letting their friends talk to them in a certain way, such as giving unflattering nicknames.

- Remind them to use "I..." messages. "I feel left out when you won't let me sit with you at lunch. Can I sit with you at lunch?"

- Teach your child that being assertive also means talking in a calm, firm tone. Stand up (or sit up) straight. Look the person in the eyes.

Part of assertive communication is learning to say "no." Tweens want to fit in and want peers to like them. Getting involved in too many activities can be overwhelming. Let them know it is okay to say, "I don't have time to join you today," or "That club isn't for me."

Key Takeaways:

- Practice effective communication skills with your child daily because they are essential to your child's academic and personal success. These skills, which take time to become proficient at, will help them be successful in their careers and lives as adults.

- Active listening and verbal and non-verbal communication can both impact the outcome of an interaction with another person.

- Being able to receive and give constructive feedback and resolve conflicts all require effective communication skills.

- Help your child understand the difference between assertive vs. aggressive communication.

Guiding your child to communicate effectively makes your parenting job easier and will impact many aspects of their life. Next, let's discuss how to help your middle schooler develop social skills that leverage their emotional intelligence and communication skills.

CHAPTER 8: SOCIAL SKILLS AND RELATIONSHIPS

"Friendship is the hardest thing in the world to explain. It's not something you learn in school. But if you haven't learned the meaning of friendship, you really haven't learned anything."

— *Muhammad Ali*

While helping your child develop emotional intelligence and communication skills, let's apply those to helping your child develop social skills. Social connections and friendships are exceedingly important for middle school students. Friends and peers can greatly impact your child's emotional well-being and success in school.

Many children find the transition to middle school overwhelming. Their routines abruptly change, and they will meet new people and make new friends, which can be difficult. While trying to find their crowd and fit in, your child might be afraid of rejection, and they may even experience anxiety because of it.

Enhance Social Connections and Friendships

Your child will need good social skills their entire life. Good social skills will give them the ability to communicate with other people in different settings easily and comfortably. Furthermore, these skills will help your child connect and relate to others. However, it might be challenging for every tween to find their place amongst people. And as a parent, it can be heartbreaking and frustrating when your child struggles to fit into different social settings. However, you can help them navigate social interactions and form meaningful relationships.

1. Have your child join groups, whether at school or in the community, that focus on what your child is interested in. They will likely feel more relaxed around people they have something in common with.

2. Encourage your child to volunteer. They will interact with people with the same interests as they do, meet and form relationships with people from different backgrounds, develop empathy, and build self-esteem as they make a positive difference in the community.

3. As discussed in Chapter 7, Effective Communication Skills, continue to help your child develop effective communication skills, including practicing active listening. As discussed in Chapter 4 - Build Resilience and Flexibility, encourage your child to reject negative self-talk and thoughts, which can hinder their ability to form relationships with others. Teach them how to question those thoughts and rephrase them.

4. As discussed in Chapter 3, Foster Independence and Self-Confidence, please continue to help your child focus on their strengths, accept who they are, and not compare themselves to others.

5. Teach your child to be actively engaged in a relationship to maintain it. They must try to spend time with their friends and be genuinely interested in their friends' actions, thoughts, and feelings.

6. As discussed in Chapter 6, Emotional Intelligence, remind your child to practice self-regulation. When angry, they need to take a step back, determine the problem, empathize with the other person, and then figure out solutions.

7. Let your child know they will meet people who are different. Talk to them about embracing people from cultures, ethnic groups, and belief systems different from theirs. Not only will this help them thrive in middle and high school, it will also help them succeed in the real world.

8. Teach your child to ask inviting questions or small talk to keep a conversation going with newly met people.

9. Role-play different situations. For example, pretend you are someone your child doesn't get along with. This can help you understand how your child sees the other person. Have your child talk to you, and then reverse roles.

Make and Maintain Social Connections

Making friends and maintaining those friendships can be hard for your tween as their school and extracurricular life gets busier. However, you can help them understand the importance of social connections with other children who may or may not be their friends. Here's how you can assist them with this.

1. Review social cues and nonverbal communication with your child. Remind them about personal space. Other social cues are facial expressions, body language, and tone of voice. Practice all these social cues with your child.

2. While discussing social cues, discuss some of the social rules they should consider. For example, they should remember to take turns talking with their friends and not dominate the conversation. Practice active listening, which includes paying attention to nonverbal communication.

3. Explain to your child that not all friends are the same. One friend might be fun to hang out with but can't keep secrets. Another friend might be a good listener but likes to do different things than your child does. Remind your child that just because a person isn't going to end up being their best friend doesn't mean that the person can't be a regular friend.

4. Please remind your child that they want to consider people with good values when looking for potential friends. For example, they won't want to be friends with someone who lies often.

5. Enroll your child in clubs and groups that support their interests, such as drama, art, soccer, singing, dancing, etc. They will find it easier to initiate and participate in conversations with people who share their interests.

6. Talk about things that can ruin friendships, like talking over people, interrupting, talking nonstop, or gossiping about others.

7. Please remind your child that sometimes both they and their friend will need space. They will need time alone or to hang out with other people.

8. Be involved with your child's relationships. Volunteer to drive them to the movies or host a movie night at your house.

9. Let your child know that they can talk to you. Actively listen to your child without judgment. Validate their feelings, and only advise if it's asked for.

Help Your Child Understand Group Dynamics and Social Skills

Cliques are a massive part of the social scene in schools. People group themselves based on their interests, how they dress, or even if they have been friends since kindergarten. Cliques can make life hard for both the people in a clique and those on the outside. This can make you want to pull your hair out in frustration because you don't know how to help your child deal with these social circles. Take a deep breath. You got this. I will guide you through these easy steps:

1. Talk about your experiences with cliques. Discuss how they made you feel about yourself and other people. Tell them how you dealt with the situation and invite them to talk about what you did right or could have done better.

2. Help them see rejection differently. Remind them of a time when they were angry or frustrated and rejected a friend or family member. Ask them to consider whether this lasted a long time or was temporary.

3. Explain the difference between healthy and unhealthy relationships and friendships. Ask them to explain what a one-sided or fake relationship looks like.

4. Ask them to name the leader of a clique your child is interested in. Then, ask them how they think that person feels. Explain that often, the leaders of those groups are insecure and worry at least as much as other people about whether they are popular and if they are going to stay popular.

5. Have your child read a book about people who overcame rejection, such as *Blubber* by Judy Blume. If your tween is mature enough, they can watch movies like *Mean Girls and Clueless.*

Sometimes, the problem isn't that a clique is excluding your child. Your child may be a part of a clique. If this is the case, dealing with the situation immediately is important. Here's how you can bring awareness to your child:

1. Ask why your child feels like they should be in a clique and what makes them want to be a part of it.

2. Talk to your child about how those outside the clique feel and how they are treated. Do other people ignore them? Are they bullied?

3. Tell your child it's essential to know the difference between spending time with friends and purposely excluding people.

4. Ask your child what they would do if the group leader wanted them to be mean to someone else or do something that they didn't want to do.

5. Talk to your child about what they had to give up to join the group and whether it was worth it.

6. Encourage your child to stand up for others who are being bullied. Also, talk to them about not participating in any bullying, whether it is talking about people behind their backs, tripping them, or any other kind of unkind behavior.

7. Remind your child that if the group members are true friends, they will respect your child's opinions, feelings, and interests.

8. Explain that cliques can change quickly. It is more important to form friendships with people with whom they can be themselves.

Manage Peer Pressure and Bullying

Peer pressure can be both positive and negative. It can encourage your child to learn new skills, develop their strengths, and increase their interest in different subjects. However, it can also have negative effects. Your child could be pressured into skipping classes, using drugs or alcohol, cheating, engaging in inappropriate online activities, and more.

Bullying is another issue middle schoolers have to deal with. In the past, it was physical and emotional bullying at school, and children at least had a reprieve at home. However, now, with technology, there's no escape. Peer pressure and bullying can get out of control if not promptly dealt with. You can help your child handle them with ease. Below are some proven strategies.

Strategies to Handle Peer Pressure

Children often give in to peer pressure because they want to fit in. They fear that they will be bullied or ignored if they don't follow along. You can't protect them from peer pressure. However, you can help them deal with it and say no. Here are some simple ways to help them deal with it.

1. Talk to your child about things happening around them, and then, based on this, tell them what is right and wrong.

2. Based on the last point, ask your children about things that their friends or some people in their circle are associated with. Once they answer, you will know the influence your child is being exposed to. You can tell them what habits are not healthy or/or dangerous, like smoking weed, vaping, skipping school, cheating, browsing adult content, etc. Then, ask your middle schooler to avoid or minimize interactions as much as possible.

3. Teach your child to firmly say no when those try to pressure your child to do something that is unhealthy or not age-appropriate. Role play and create situations where it's one-on-one or a group of people.

4. Encourage your child to spend time with other children who don't give in to peer pressure. It's easier for them to stand up for themselves when they feel someone has their back.

5. Encourage your child to talk to you about the situation, but also a teacher or guidance counselor.

6. Know who your child's friends are. If there is a situation you are concerned about, reach out to their parents.

7. As discussed in Chapter 3, Foster Independence and Self-Confidence, help your child develop positive self-confidence and self-esteem. They will be less likely to give in to peer pressure.

Recognize and Deal with Bullying

There are different types of bullying. Physical bullying involves hitting, kicking, tripping, and being forced to do things they don't want to do. Verbal bullying includes name-calling, threats, or gestures. Relational bullying is when the victim is deliberately ignored, trashing their reputation, posting mean comments online, or sharing embarrassing images. Another form of bullying is when victims' belongings are purposely damaged or destroyed.

Bullying can happen anywhere: At school, on the bus, on social media, in gaming communities, and in text messages. It is the worst thing that can happen to children, leading to severe consequences. It can lead to low self-esteem, depression, anxiety, self-harm, drug use, alcohol abuse, and even suicide. There are other effects as well, including insomnia, bedwetting, headaches, and stomach aches. It can also lead to poor academic performance.

Bullying is terrifying. However, you can help your child deal with bullying. Start by knowing the signs of bullying.

- Unexplainable injuries

- Lost belongings -- especially if it happens often

- Frequent headaches or stomach aches.

- Feeling sick or faking being sick.

- Change in eating habits

- Trouble sleeping

- Nightmares

- Declining grades

- Loss of interest in school or other activities

- Loss of friends

- Feelings of hopelessness

- Decrease in self-esteem

- Self-destructive behaviors -- self-harm, suicidal ideation, drug use, alcohol use, running away

How can you help your child avoid getting bullied? Based on actual circumstances, you can choose from these tips.

- Talk to your child every day about what happened at school. Ask them about interactions they had with other people. When your child gets used to talking to you about their day, they will be more likely to open up to you if they get bullied.

- If your child comes to you, praise them for coming to you and never try to shut them down.

- Reassure your child that they aren't alone.

- Point out that the bully's behavior is unacceptable and assure them that you feel no child should be bullied. Once they know your view, they will likely open up.

- Even if your child comes to you about bullying or seeing someone getting bullied, instead of letting them take the wrong idea, assure them that the one getting bullied, be it your own child or someone they know, has not done anything wrong.

- After learning about their complaints and the things they see or endure at school, contact the principal as soon as possible and let them know what is going on. Ask the principal what steps they will take to rectify the situation. Check in with your child and the principal often to ensure the problem is handled. If it's not, take the issue to the superintendent.

- If threats have been made or your child is physically hurt, get the police and school authority figures involved immediately.

- Advise your child to use the buddy system when going to their locker or in the area where the bully is.

- Have your child practice not reacting. Bullies are looking for some reaction, whether it is anger or crying. Teach them to count to ten, write down their feelings, take a deep breath, and walk away. Let your child know that laughing or smiling might provoke the bully into doing something worse.

- When the bully starts, tell them to stop and walk away.

Sometimes, your child is the bully. You can help your child realize that his or her behavior is unacceptable and must be stopped immediately.

1. Talk to your child about the reasons why people bully others. Ask them to explain why they bully other people.

2. Ask your child to put themselves in their victim's shoes and explain how they think their victim feels.

3. Let them know that their behavior is unacceptable and harmful.

4. Ensure your child knows there will be consequences if the bullying continues.

5. Model respectful behavior. Your child is watching you. If you talk to a waiter, cashier, or other person disrespectfully, your child will imitate you.

Key Takeaways

- Get your child involved in groups, clubs, and other organizations that your child might be interested in. It's a great way to foster social connections and build friendships.

- Ask your child what they want from a friendship and how they can be a good friend to others.

- Talk to your tweens about peer pressure and how they can avoid dangerous or unethical situations.

- Watch for signs of bullying. Help your child learn how to stand up to bullies by telling them to stop and simply walking away.

- Model respectful behavior.

- Let your child know that you are always there for them when they need to talk or if they get into a dangerous situation.

Social interactions, friendship, peer pressure, and bullying are tough topics. However, you and your child will get through the tough times and thrive when you work together. Now stretch, breathe, and get ready to learn about some other essential skills for your child to develop.

PART 4: GUIDE AND SUPPORT YOUR CHILD IN DEVELOPING ESSENTIAL LIFE & ACADEMIC SKILLS

CHAPTER 9: ESSENTIAL LIFE SKILLS FOR TWEENS

"Life skills develop the right attitudes to think smartly, act smartly, and to live consciously."

— *Rajeev Ranjan*

As much as social skills are necessary for your tweens, some essential life and academic skills are equally important. With rapid technological advancement, students are expected to acquire more information in school. Nowadays, schools are primarily about passing tests, getting ready for high school, and paving the foundation for college applications. Many important life skills should be taught or emphasized at school and at home because these skills are critical to our children's well-being, now and in the future. There are plenty of teen life skills resources out there. I want to summarize the essential skills that involve your support to help your tween quickly develop them. It will also make your parenting job easier once your tween acquires these critical life skills.

Practical Skills: Healthy Cooking

There are hundreds of different life skills that your child will need to know besides getting a solid education. Helping your child learn these basic yet essential skills can be rewarding and fun. Meanwhile, these skills are essential for several reasons:

- Prepare your child for real life when they have to look after themselves.

- Increase self-confidence.

- Teach them how to be responsible.

- Develop independence as they learn how to perform tasks on their own.

- Fosters decision-making skills as they learn to prioritize tasks and determine how to accomplish them.

Unless your child foresees meals consisting of Ramen, microwave dinners, and takeout, they have to learn how to cook. Numerous recipes are available. We want to focus on helping your child learn, explore easy and healthy cooking, and have fun with you while learning.

1. Start by asking them to help you create a healthy menu high in protein, moderate in healthy fats, rich in fiber, minerals, and vitamins, and moderate in carbs.

2. Have your child figure out what ingredients are needed for each menu item. This means they will have to read a recipe from you or recipe books.

3. Allow your child to go shopping with you. This is a great time to teach them to read labels and evaluate ways to source healthy ingredients.

4. It is also the perfect time to teach them about budgeting.

5. Teach them cooking safety, such as where to place the handle on pans, how to use a potholder, how to control the temperature to prevent burning, and how to not leave the stove unattended. Also, teach them what to do if there is a fire.

6. Remind them to wash their hands before they prepare food; don't mix the cutting knife and board for cutting raw meat with those for cutting fruits and vegetables.

7. Explain that they must put all the food ingredients and condiments they will need on the counter and tools such as measuring spoons, cups, spatulas, etc. Ask them, "What tools do you think we will need?"

8. Praise them even if they forget something, and gently remind them.

9. Show them how to prepare different ingredients safely, including knife safety and using a potato peeler without skinning their fingers.

10. Guide them on the sequential steps, especially those requiring more precise measurements.

11. The next time your child cooks the same dish, try to be more hands-off. Let them practice cooking and gently remind them if they make a mistake.

Practical Skills: Cleaning

Clutter and messes look terrible and can prevent you and your child from focusing. Teaching your child to clean and keep their study and living spaces organized helps them become more responsible, develop self-discipline, and create a sense of accomplishment when they are done. So, use these guidelines to introduce the habit of cleanliness in your children.

1. Explain that a clean area is a healthy area. Talk to your child about bugs, ants, mice, and even mold that can show up in a messy room or house. You can also talk about the hazards of a mess, such as tripping over something.

2. Talk to them about organizing their belongings and room. Ask, "How will you find your favorite shirt when your clothes are thrown all over your room?"

3. Show them how to do laundry, run the dishwasher, and clean the bathroom.

4. Assign your child weekly chores, including keeping their room clean and helping clean the kitchen and other living areas where they leave their items behind.

5. Take before and after cleaning pictures to show the contrast and incentivize them to repeat the routine.

6. Reward them with an allowance if they do a great job and help them learn how to manage money.

I have heard parents ask this question - should they pay their children to do chores, such as cleaning? Instilling the principle in your child that cleaning is part of their personal and family responsibilities can benefit their lifetime. But if you ask your child to do something out of the ordinary, children, anyone, respond positively to rewards. As long as your child doesn't feel entitled to payments for cleaning after themselves and helping the family out, you can decide on a bonus in the form of a cash reward if your child consistently does an excellent job in cleaning or does something out of the ordinary.

Practical Skills: Safety Practices

Teaching safety and basic first aid is essential. It is more like a need; every parent should teach their children about safety and basic first aid. These safety procedures are more than what they learn at school. By mastering these essential safety tips, your tween can give you peace of mind and help take care of their younger siblings.

1. They likely already know about looking both ways before they cross a road, but it never hurts to remind them. And do not look at their phones or music players while crossing the street.

2. They should always wear helmets when biking, roller skating, and riding scooters. Remind them to follow all the safety protocols explained when attending friends' birthday parties at recreational facilities.

3. Stay alert when they walk or jog alone. Do not converse with a total stranger when no other people are in sight.

4. Remind your child that if they are ever on fire or somehow catch it, ask them to stop, drop, and roll to put it out.

5. Practice fire drills in the house and give each person an assignment. For example, your child's job is to get out of the home as fast as possible and call 9-1-1. Your job is to ensure everyone gets out safely and puts out the fire if possible. Make sure your child knows all exits, even windows.

6. Practice safety protocols to prepare for natural disasters (e.g., earthquakes, floods, snowstorms, etc.)

7. If they see a weapon of any form, notify an adult and do not touch or test any weapon.

8. Ensure your child knows where the first aid kit is and how to administer basic first aid, such as cleaning out a scrape or cut, using antibiotic ointment, and using a band-aid. Remind them to find you or another adult if they, or someone else, has a more serious injury.

9. Do not take any medication on their own without asking or confirming with you first.

Practical Skills: Personal Finance Basics

Your child already knows that money can buy things that they want. However, they need to learn how to manage their money and budget. And this doesn't have to be complex financial literacy. It's mainly about making responsible decisions and managing and spending money wisely.

Instilling money management concepts in your child will benefit your child and make your parenting job easier. Your tween won't keep nagging you to buy things outside your budget; they will appreciate their parents more for providing food, shelter, clothes, and toys and be more motivated to help parents with chores. This learning process might inspire your child to develop entrepreneurial ideas about making money as they get older.

Plenty of wonderful personal finance books exist for teens, an older age group. I want to make it easy for you by highlighting and simplifying critical personal finance concepts that you can explain to your child to help them get ahead of the curve, making your life easier now and down the road.

Household Budgeting

- Show your child how you manage your budget every month, emphasizing that bills and other obligations are taken care of first.

- Talk about the difference between needs and wants. "We need to keep the lights on and food in the kitchen. We want to go to the movies. We have to take care of the needs before the wants." State such examples to help them learn the difference.

Spending

- Talk to them about impulse buying. Remind them when shopping that if they buy a video game, they may not have enough money for the shoes they need. They are old enough to weigh the pros and cons of buying the video game and make a decision.

- When your tween is considering making an impulsive buy, have them wait at least a day before they purchase anything. The item will still be available the next day, and they will have time to really consider whether they want it.

- Show them coupons and reward points you collect so they can be savvy shoppers and get into the habit of looking for deals.

- Please explain to them never spend above means, although your child might have seen you use credit cards to make purchases.

Allowance & Earning

- To prevent children from feeling entitled to receiving money from parents, consider giving them an allowance as a reward for doing chores well and helping out around the house. Let them know what they will earn for each job.

- Show your child that recycling plastic bottles is good for the environment, and they can earn and keep the money from recycling.

- Please encourage them to find other ways to earn money, such as helping you with a garage sale, selling their unused toys and bikes online, or doing light yard work for neighbors.

Savings & Passive Income

- Help them set savings goals. If they want a game system, they must save up for it.

- Teach them to balance how they handle money. For example, use the 50-30-20 rule or a variation thereof. Thirty percent of any money they get should be automatically put into savings. Fifty percent is set aside for spending. The other twenty percent is for donating to charities, the church, or people in need. Of course, they are always encouraged to put more into savings, especially if there is something big that they want to buy. Another way of dividing their money is fifty percent for things they need (such as a dress or expensive shoes), thirty percent on what they want (such as going to the movies), and twenty percent for savings.

- Explain the different bank options that tweens can use to collect passive income – interests! Savings accounts can earn interest and allow account holders to withdraw anytime. CD that might earn higher interest but can't withdraw from the account at any time.

- Explain why having multiple bank accounts is necessary: a checking account for paying bills, one or two savings accounts for collecting passive income, and building an emergency fund.

- Introduce the simple yet super powerful money concept – leveraging compounded growth - a simple way of introducing them to investing and a fun way of applying math to our daily lives.

Compounding Works in Our Favor:

For example, a $100 deposit in a high-interest account can receive $5.00 of interest at the end of year one if the annual interest of your child's savings or CD account is 5% and there is no withdrawal from this account during the year. The balance at the beginning of year two is $105. By the end of year two, if the interest rate remains 5% and your child didn't withdraw any money during year two, their $105 earns $5.25 of interest. The account balance is $110.25 at the end of year two. In just two years, your child's passive income is $10.25, which is 10.25% of growth! That's the power of compounding. Money, in this case, can grow on trees without your tween doing anything!

You can introduce the concept of paying taxes on any earnings (passive or active) later when they are old enough to get a job and receive paychecks. For now, the focus is on understanding the importance of saving and how to leverage compounding to earn passive income.

<u>Compounding Works Against Us:</u>

Here, you can extend the concept of compounded interest to using credit cards. If we don't pay down our credit card balances in a timely fashion, credit card interest compounds even faster, causing people to be in greater debt. This further explains the previous spending tip — why we don't spend above our means. Borrowing too much without having the means to pay off our credit card balances causes people to be in greater debt.

Money Management

- Use a child-friendly money management app or their bank mobile account app to help your child manage their money. Encourage them to track deposits, spending, and withdrawals.

- Please encourage your child to make a specific budget for their spending each month and define a savings goal each month or each year.

Giving Back

- Teach them about giving back, whether it is to a church or a charity. They will feel good about themselves for helping another person.

- The universe has an interesting way of encouraging giving back. When we genuinely give something to others without expecting anything in return, we receive something beneficial in other forms and shapes.

Practical Skills: Good Manners

It seems that manners are in short supply these days. "Gimme" has replaced "Please." However, you can help your child learn manners that they will use to show respect to others and will help them earn respect.

Below are some basic and essential manners that you can teach or demonstrate to your child:

- Teach them or remind them of the Golden Rule — "Treat others as you would like others to treat you," or "Do not treat others in ways that you would not like to be treated."

- Apologize and be accountable for mistakes.

- Ask for permission before they touch other people's belongings. This even includes when they are with their friends. For example, they should ask before grabbing a pencil from their friend's bag.

- Refrain from texting or answering their phone when they are talking to someone.

- Make eye contact when talking to other people.

- Say "excuse me" when they interrupt a conversation. They should also say "excuse me" when they bump into someone else.

- Say "please," "could you please," "would you please," and "thank you" when asking others for help.

- Cover their mouth with their elbow when they sneeze or cough.

- Chew with their mouth closed and don't talk with their mouth full.

- Don't reach across the dinner table.

- Wait their turn to talk. Don't talk over people or interrupt.

- Write thank you emails or notes after receiving gifts.

- Stay polite and cordial, and use appropriate language when talking to others, even if your child disagrees.

- Don't ignore someone's greetings, even if your child dislikes that person.

- Hold the door for someone behind them.

Teaching your child manners is an ongoing process. You must remind them and correct them when they forget these basic manners. However, stay patient and don't get frustrated when they make a mistake. Mistakes will help them learn even more. Meanwhile, during this ongoing process of learning, look closely into these points:

- Make sure your child knows what is expected of them.

- Dole out consequences if you need to. For example, if they forget to say please even after being reminded, don't acknowledge their request.

- Explain why it's essential to have good manners.

- Give your middle schooler more chances to practice good manners in public. For example, have them politely ask the waiter for more water or talk to the cashier when purchasing.

- Role-play different scenarios where they should use good manners.

- Watch a television show or movie and discuss the characters' manners or lack of manners.

- Praise your child for using good manners.

Once your child masters the basic manners listed above, you can introduce them to events or venue-specific manners, such as attending weddings, graduation ceremonies, semi-formals, etc.

Practical Skills: Community Engagement

Raising socially responsible children who are engaged in their community is vital. Once they have it, they learn how to be respectful and demonstrate empathy. It also helps them to understand and value diversity. Furthermore, they will be able to form healthy relationships with others. However, there are different ways that you can instill these important values in your child.

1. You can model social responsibility and community involvement. Let your child see you giving back to society by volunteering, doing community service, or even picking up trash in the park.

2. Have your children donate some of their used items and things that are close to their hearts. This will also introduce them to empathy and kindness.

3. Please encourage your child to donate part of their earnings to a cause they believe in. Alternatively, they can donate it to someone in need by buying groceries or other necessities.

4. Teach your child to recycle as much as possible.

5. Explain the importance of supporting local businesses (e.g., buying from the local farmers' market).

6. Talk to your child about being kind and respectful to everyone. Ask them always to consider how their words and actions impact others.

7. Teach your child to be accountable for their actions. Remind them that it is better to admit when they make a mistake and take the consequences than to lie about it or, worse, blame it on someone else. Being accountable will earn them respect.

8. If you belong to a church, encourage your child to become active in the church. They can teach a lesson to the littles, sing in the choir, or even help with cleaning.

Key Takeaways

- Teach your child healthy cooking by letting them plan their favorite dinner, shop for healthy ingredients, and prepare them. Alternatively, start with something simple and work up to more complex dishes.

- Remind your child that being clean is important to good physical and mental health.

- Go over safety tips with your child. Practice fire drills often in your home. Make sure your child knows where the first aid kit is and how to use different products.

- Encourage your child to do chores and allow your child to earn money by doing chores.

- Teach them how to budget and save, as well as how to spend wisely. Expose them to concepts of earning and collecting passive income.

- Explain why good manners are important and let your child know that you expect them always to use good manners.

- Teach the importance of social responsibility. Please encourage your child to get involved in their community and give back.

- Remember that modeling is the strongest teaching tool.

Please relax for a moment and digest all that you've learned in this chapter. Then, get ready to learn how to help your middle schooler grasp the slippery rope of time management.

CHAPTER 10: TIME MANAGEMENT AND GOAL SETTING

"A plan is what; a schedule is when. It takes both a plan and a schedule to get things done."

— *Peter Turla*

It's tiring for any parent to keep reminding their child to get ready for school, finish homework, do chores, and go to bed on time daily. It's stressful for many parents to see their children with no desire to achieve goals or have lofty goals but don't know how to achieve them. While your middle schooler may think it's OK to wait until the last minute to complete their science project or math homework, procrastination can lead to lower academic performance and more stress for your tween and you.

Tweens who don't learn and acquire time management skills are at risk of becoming lifelong procrastinators. Waiting until the last minute to get things could cause problems ranging from high-stress levels at work to relationship issues later in life. Their college professors or future bosses aren't likely to accept late work —or the excuses for delayed projects. So, it's important to teach or model to your tween how to manage time wisely and behave responsibly. That means proactively managing their time without requiring constant reminders or assistance to get their work done.

Let's discuss how to help your child acquire time management and goal-setting skills to live a productive life and reduce stress for you and your child.

Schedule and Prioritize Tasks with Your Tween

Let's explore the fundamental importance of creating a daily or weekly schedule. Further in this section, we'll discuss the art of identifying and prioritizing tasks — distinguishing between what's truly important and merely urgent. Alongside practical tips, we'll introduce scheduling tools and apps suitable for tweens, making the process effective and engaging.

Teach Time Management Skills

Each child's inner thought process is different. Many feel overwhelming pressure to earn good grades, fit in socially, or reach a particular standard of excellence in competitive activities like sports, while others suffer from low motivation that may point to anxiety or depression. You want to avoid introducing time management as one more mountain you expect them to climb. Instead, you can describe it as a skill they will find empowering in managing the pressures they face every day. Using time wisely also makes space for self-care, which helps your tween maintain a healthy balance.

Here are some steps you can take to teach your tween essential time management skills:

- **Advise your tween to write down their schedule.** Your tween's time may easily get taken up with video games or social media if they are not careful. Teach them to schedule their day so they can set aside time for chores, homework, and other responsibilities. Encourage them to schedule free time so time doesn't idly pass without feeling like they have not done anything fun.

- **Set time limits, but avoid constant nagging.** It can be tempting to nag your tween or offer repeat reminders. But, telling your tween to do their homework or chores repeatedly reduces their sense of taking responsibility. Set rules about your expectations and follow through with consequences when necessary. Or use technology such as setting an alarm on mobile phones or Amazon Alexa to set time limits for your child to complete each task. Your child at this age will likely pay more attention to an alarm sound from a digital device or a reminder from an AI-based voice than the nagging voice of her own parents.

- **Encourage your tween to develop routines.** Encourage your tween to establish healthy habits, such as no more snacking after 8:30 pm, finishing homework by 9 pm the latest so they could go to bed at a reasonable time. Then, ask them to prepare their backpack for the next day before bed. Remember to floss after brushing your teeth, before bed, etc. Once they get into the routine of doing things in a certain order at predictable times, they won't get distracted so easily or squander time.

- **Provide your tween with easily accessible time management tools.**
Whether it's a digital or physical calendar, a planner that your tween
writes everything in, or an app that manages your tween's schedule, it
helps your tween find the tools that will work best for them. Please talk
about the importance of creating a schedule and using lists to prioritize
their time wisely.

- **Help them limit online time.** Your tween may waste hours on social
media or video games unless you introduce healthy media habits. The
American Academy of Pediatrics offers a family media plan that helps
you set standards for everyone in the household. This reinforces the idea
that adults and kids must manage their digital media use.

Help Your Tween Prioritize Activities

It's common for tweens to have conflicts in their schedules. A basketball game,
birthday party, and church activity may all coincide. Talk to your tween about
prioritizing activities based on his interests and the importance of his goals, values,
and commitments.

Helping your child with time management and priorities is another way of encouraging self-management and goal-setting. As your child takes on more academic responsibility, participates in more extracurriculars, and desires to hang out
with friends, work with him to set priorities and map out his time.

Encourage Perseverance and Celebrating Achievements

Perseverance is critical to achieving goals. We'll emphasize its importance and
provide strategies for parents to help their tweens stay focused. Celebrating small
wins is equally essential to boost your tween's motivation and foster a resilient
mindset.

Help Tweens Set SMART Goals

Setting goals is an essential step in achieving success. For tweens, setting SMART
goals can be especially helpful in reaching their targets. By creating goals using
the SMART framework, tweens can ensure that they are specific and measurable,
making it easier to track their progress.

Additionally, making goals relevant to their lives and setting a time limit helps
keep tweens motivated and accountable. By following these tips in creating
SMART goals, your tween can set themselves up for success! A SMART goal

is a goal that is specific, measurable, attainable, relevant, and time-bound. This acronym can help tweens remember the key components of effective goal setting.

Specific

When setting a specific goal, you can ask your tween to answer the following questions: What are you trying to accomplish? Who or what is involved? What do you want to achieve? Where will it take place? Which requirements and constraints might you run into?

Measurable

The goal itself should be quantifiable, and your tween should be able to measure progress towards it. This means that tweens should be able to track their progress and see whether they are getting closer to or further away from their target.

Attainable

Goals should challenge tweens but still be achievable. If a goal is too easy, it likely won't provide much motivation. On the other hand, if a goal is impossible to reach, it can lead to discouragement. You can guide your team by asking them what you must do to accomplish your goal. For instance, if you are a couch potato, it might be unrealistic to have the goal of running a marathon in 3 months. However, setting a goal to run a 5k is realistically aggressive.

Relevant

Smaller or short-term goals should relate to realizing your tween's bigger or longer-term goals and align with their values. By setting relevant goals, tweens will have more clarity about why they are trying to achieve these goals and will be more motivated to achieve them.

Time-Bound

Putting a time limit on a goal helps ensure that it gets done. With a deadline, it is easy to work towards a goal. You can help your tween raise awareness of the time limit by asking when you will finish this goal.

Setting SMART goals is a skill that will benefit your child in their personal and professional lives down the road. Additionally, by setting SMART goals, tweens have a better sense of which direction they are heading toward and learn how to prioritize their time and resources better. After they achieve their goals, they can be proud of their accomplishments.

Key Takeaways

- Explain to your tween about the importance of time and discipline.

- Guide your tween in time management.

- Understand why goals are integral for children; every child should have a list of goals they want to achieve.

- Help your child set SMART goals.

- Celebrate small or any progress that will motivate your tween to work towards their goals, big or small.

This chapter taught you the importance of time management and goal setting. Furthermore, it shows how to instill such abilities in our tweens, help them understand different types of goals, and motivate them to reach goals by teaching them the importance of goals. This chapter was a great learning experience, and so will the next chapter, which will focus on academic success skills.

CHAPTER 11: ACADEMIC SUCCESS

"Education is the passport to the future, for tomorrow belongs to those who prepare for it today."

— Malcolm X

While guiding your child to develop time management skills and set goals for anything they want to achieve as the foundation, it is time to ensure they have essential academic skills and the right mindset to succeed at school. It all starts by motivating them to set academic SMART goals introduced in the previous chapter.

Guide Your Tween to Set Academic SMART Goals

Encouraging tweens to set academic SMART goals is a beneficial way to enhance their success in school. SMART goals are Specific, Measurable, Achievable, Relevant, and Time-bound. To motivate tweens, parents can initiate discussions about academic aspirations, whether improving grades or participating in contests.

Guiding tweens to make their goals specific, such as aiming to raise a math grade from a C to a B, ensures clarity and focus. Making measurable goals allows tweens to track progress through grade improvements or contest preparation.

Goals should also be achievable and relevant to their academic success and interests. Setting deadlines provides structure and encourages accountability. By engaging tweens in setting SMART academic goals, parents support their academic journey and instill valuable skills for future success.

Encourage Effective Study Habits - Plan and Stay Organized

Developing good study habits requires teaching tweens effective strategies, especially when unsure how much supervision to provide. Studying entails more than reviewing notes; it's about organizing tasks, understanding what to study and when, and tracking assignments and tests.

While online platforms like Schoology offer some support, tweens need to personalize their study plans. They can use the platform to access daily assignments and grades and create individualized action plans for each subject's assignments, tests, and projects. This approach fosters independence and cultivates essential study skills.

- **Create a calendar**. Show tweens how to use a large wall calendar and a set of markers to keep track of all the assignments. They can assign each class a different colored marker and write all of their assignments, activities, and appointments on the calendar. Or they can use an online calendar — and sync it with multiple devices, including their smartphone and laptop.

- **Plan for test preparation at least one week ahead.** Tweens can break down information on the calendar to make a study plan for each week, especially when tests are coming up. Furthermore, show them how to transfer obligations for each week from the big calendar to a weekly planner, ensuring time to work on each assignment and start preparing for tests no matter how confident they are a few days before it's due. Or have them print out a weekly list from their online calendar.

- **Create a daily checklist.** It may seem overkill, but breaking down the weekly plan into a daily checklist can also be very helpful. This to-do list helps kids keep track of their day and see how much progress they're making. It's a good idea for kids to list each day's tasks in the order they should be done and to write down the specific time of each class or appointment.

Checklist Method of Studying

Once your middle schoolers know what to study, the next step is learning how to study. This can be broken into a checklist where your tween can tick out the things they have studied, and they can keep track of what's remaining.

- **Follow instructions and class notes.** Do homework and practice as instructed by each teacher. If your tween has a math assignment to finish 20 problems, don't skip a few math problems. There is a reason for every assignment.

- **Establish rewards**. At first, you may need to help kids set up a reward system. For example, for every chapter they read, you might let them use their digital device for 5 minutes. Eventually, they'll learn to reward themselves, even just by having a snack between English and algebra homework.

- **Create a study checklist.** This includes all the steps kids need to take to get ready for homework and what they need to study that day. Having everything listed out can make it easier for them to get started and prioritize their time. It may also make their homework load less overwhelming.

- **Keep a worry pad or a journal.** A worry pad is a tool for tweens who are easily distracted by their thoughts. Instead of dealing with all the distracting things that keep popping into their heads, they can write them down on the pad. When they're done studying, they can deal with what distracts them.

Encourage Your Tween to Develop Note-Taking Skills

Starting middle school, regardless of public or private schools, teachers expect students to become more self-sufficient, meaning not having teachers repeat assignment details or nag students to turn in homework. Your tweens have different teachers for different subjects. They may not have the opportunity to run into teachers from the first period on the same day. Sometimes, teachers are too busy to enter assignments and test dates into the online platform on time. So, students should also use what they hear first-hand inside the classroom regarding assignment details and due dates.

Even adults who attend five different meetings a day at work can't keep track of action items from every meeting without taking notes. So, helping your child develop and improve note-taking skills is important for staying organized, turning in assignments on time with quality, and not getting overwhelmed by back-to-back tests. This is also a crucial academic skill for them in high school and a life skill beyond school. Good note-taking requires:

1). Listening skills

2). Clear and concise writing skills.

You might think that you are not the greatest note-taker yourself, and that's fine. Every strategy and tip we discussed in this book does not require you to master it before you can encourage, cultivate, or teach your child if you can. The point is to increase your awareness of what can be done early and utilize opportunities and available resources to help your child.

Help Your Tween Ease Test-Taking Anxiety

We discussed how to help your tween build self-confidence in Chapter 3 and manage stress in Chapter 5. These are critical skills that can help your child deal with test-taking anxiety.

Help Your Tween Bounce Back from Academic Setbacks

In Chapter 4, we discussed how to help your tween build resilience. That general resilience ability you helped your tween develop applies to academic setbacks such as failing a test or not winning a debate contest.

Navigate Academic Challenges and Support

Middle school academic rigor is usually a big step up from elementary school. Every tween encounters a unique set of challenges. Parents must recognize their child's academic challenges early and find resources to support their child.

Our self-perception during childhood and adolescence forms the basis of our self-worth, influencing our ability to harness intelligence and find happiness. Negative experiences like bullying or academic struggles can erode self-belief, leading to self-doubt and anxiety.

Perfectionism, exacerbated by social media, is prevalent among youth, driven by fear of failure and the pressure to meet unrealistic standards. Despite appearing positive, perfectionist behaviors stem from anxiety and can have detrimental effects on mental health.

Addressing these challenges requires fostering healthy self-esteem and promoting resilience to overcome obstacles. It's crucial to recognize the impact of societal pressures and prioritize mental well-being in today's youth.

How Do We Help Them?

The good news is that you have learned many strategies and tips from the previous chapters, which have already paved the foundation for you to help your child overcome many academic challenges stemming from their mindset by developing their resilience, self-confidence, emotional intelligence, independent problem-solving, time management, and goal-setting skills.

In parallel, seek support from the school and parent network. Seek resources at your child's middle school, online, or local community for academic support or activities. Seek support from parental networks and crowdsource solutions.

Before I conclude on the importance of our parental role, allow me to share a story about Thomas Edison, one of the greatest inventors of all time. In the late 1800s, Thomas was asked to leave his school for being perceived as mentally ill and a challenging child to manage in the classroom. However, his mother had a different perspective. She told him that he was asked to leave the school because he was too intelligent for the school to handle and proceeded to homeschool him from that day forward. Many years later, he became one of the greatest inventors in history.

Now, if his mother had told him the truth—that he was perceived as mentally ill and challenging — would he have achieved such greatness? We'll never know for certain, but similar stories and our growing understanding of the power of our beliefs strongly suggest otherwise. What we believe about ourselves lays the foundation for both success and happiness.

This story alone highlights the importance of our roles as parents in helping our children build the foundations for a happy and fulfilling life. So, we must assist our children in becoming more resilient in a challenging world by helping them recognize their worth and value and accept themselves for who they are. Suppose your tween believes in themselves and knows that their self-worth is never a reflection of anyone else's opinion or what they can do. In that case, everything in the external world will fall into place. It all starts within them.

Prepare for High School and Beyond

When selecting high school options (public, private, online accredited, home-schooling, dual enrollment in college), relatives, friends, teachers, and siblings are quick to offer their opinions. It can feel like the weight of the world is on your shoulders. At the end of the day, you know your child and what is best for them, at least better than everyone who doesn't live with your child. There could be hundreds of different opinions when preparing your children for high school and beyond. You know your child the best and focus on what is best for your child. There is no absolutely right or wrong path.

Encourage Your Child to Pursue a Passion

Children who tend to do well in high school are those who identify and develop an area of personal interest. And let's not forget the importance of "Constructive Use of Time." Children may excel and find passion in activities that aren't often considered academic.

Although some children seem to excel at everything, it's rare and an unrealistic expectation. It's great if your child wants to challenge themselves by exploring new interests. Encourage them to pursue their true passions starting in middle school.

Avoid Unrealistic Academic Expectations

Due to technological advancements, college-level learning now permeates high school and even some middle school curricula. Many US public high schoolers tackle challenging subjects like AP Physics 1 or AP Calculus as early as 10th grade, driven by academic and peer pressures.

While early exposure to subjects like physics offers lifelong analytical skills, parents must balance academic ambitions with a well-rounded life for their tweens. Introducing physics concepts through interactive experiences, like science museums, can spark interest without pressuring tweens into advanced courses. It's essential to foster academic curiosity while ensuring tweens enjoy a balanced childhood without unrealistic expectations.

College or No College?

Believe it or not, parents can start thinking about this question while their child is in middle school because it could impact their high school course selection and extracurricular activity participation. The previous generation emphasized college or university as the preferred option for every young adult. That's no longer the case. With the rising costs associated with college, it can be an enormous investment for students from middle-class American families who don't qualify for college financial aid. With artificial intelligence replacing some jobs, a college degree does not automatically guarantee long-term financial success.

Key Takeaways

- Help your child develop good study habits and note-taking skills, set academic goals, stay organized, and manage distractions.

- Apply tips and strategies you learned in previous chapters to help your child ease test-taking anxiety and build resilience to overcome academic setbacks.

- Seek resources from school, parental networks, local, and online communities to help address academic challenges.

- Start cultivating your tween's passion and avoid setting unrealistic academic expectations, which can help your child thrive in school.

- Keep an open mind about whether your child is attending college or not down the road.

In this chapter, we learned about strategies to help your child acquire essential academic skills. The next stop is helping your child navigate the digital age.

CHAPTER 12: NAVIGATE THE DIGITAL AGE

"We may have to exercise discipline to use the controls we have but we are not slaves to these devices unless we allow ourselves to become so. To me, the trick is to put yourself in charge of your screens instead of allowing your screens to be in charge of you."

— *Dr. Edward Hallowell*

In this digitally advanced age, adults and children face information overload, device addiction, inappropriate content, and content that induces negative emotions. Children have less self-control than adults, making parenting extra challenging when you have to pull your child away from their devices to get homework done and go to bed at regular times. Take a deep breath, and let's tackle these challenges now.

Understand and Manage Digital Challenges

In the digital age, tweens face numerous challenges, including cyberbullying, digital addiction, and information overload. Parents must understand these challenges to manage them and promote healthy digital habits effectively. Digital devices offer benefits like communication and relationship-building, but they also expose tweens to cyberbullying and other harmful effects.

Open communication between parents and tweens is crucial, as it builds trust and allows for monitoring of digital device usage. Studies indicate that parental involvement significantly reduces exposure to harmful online content and internet addiction. By actively engaging in their tweens' lives and educating themselves about digital devices and social media, parents can provide the necessary support to mitigate the negative impacts of digital usage and ensure their tweens' overall well-being and development.

Cyberbullying and Online Harassment

Cyberbullying and online harassment are pervasive issues that can have serious consequences for tweens' mental health and well-being. By raising awareness and providing strategies for dealing with cyberbullying, tweens can protect themselves and support their peers in navigating online interactions safely.

What Parents Can Do When Cyberbullying Happens?

Notice - Recognize your tween's change in behavior or mood. Examine whether these changes occur when your tween is using a digital device.

Monitor — Although direct communication is best, in this situation, it is necessary to consistently check your tween's browsing history, social media sites, and apps.

Talk — Ask questions to understand what is happening and who is involved.

Document — Take photos of harmful content or posts as a way of keeping records of cyberbullying incidents.

Report — Parents can contact social media platforms or apps to report offensive content. If your child has received physical threats or is engaging in illegal behavior, they can report this to the police.

Support — Try to determine if your child may require more professional support, such as seeking the guidance of a counselor or mental health professional.

Digital Addiction and Screen Time Management

Excessive screen time and digital addiction are common concerns in today's hyper-connected world. By fostering awareness of screen time habits and implementing strategies for moderation, tweens can strike a balance between online and offline activities, promoting overall well-being and productivity.

Excessive screen time and online engagement can lead to problems like digital addiction, sleep disturbance, and reduced physical activity. Parents should encourage a healthy balance between online and offline activities and promote responsible digital use.

Navigate Information Overload and Digital Literacy

The abundance of online information can overwhelm tweens, leading to confusion and misinformation. Teaching digital literacy skills, such as critical thinking, fact-checking, and media literacy, empowers tweens to navigate the digital landscape confidently and discern credible sources from misinformation.

Ensure Internet Safety, Age-Appropriate Content, and Healthy Screen Time

Internet safety is crucial for tweens, as they face threats like identity theft and inappropriate content. Educating them about privacy settings and safe browsing empowers them to navigate the Internet responsibly. Parents should stay involved, teaching children about online risks and implementing controls.

Note that in unsupervised community channels such as Discord, it is not hard for scammers and predators to pretend to be a tween or teenager in a gaming community and start direct messaging with your child. Direct messaging between two individuals is not moderated.

If it's not feasible for you to closely monitor your child's communication channels, let your child know never to disclose any personal information, home address, real name, or parents' job, financial information, and never share personal photos with anyone on Discord, no matter how much the other party talks like a nice or flirty tween.

Managing screen time is also vital to prevent issues like sleep disturbances and reduced physical activity. Set clear boundaries and encourage outdoor activities to maintain a healthy balance between the virtual and real world.

Ensure Age-Appropriate Content:

With access to a vast array of online content, ensuring that tweens consume age-appropriate material is essential for their development and well-being. By guiding tweens towards reputable sources and discussing the importance of critical consumption, parents can help them make informed choices about the content they engage with online.

The Internet contains a wide range of content, including content unsuitable for tweens. Parents can set up content filters and monitoring tools to limit exposure to inappropriate content. It is equally important to teach children to recognize and avoid such content.

If you discover your child has already stumbled upon inappropriate content, calmly let your child know it's not age-appropriate and that there is alternative educational or entertainment content that is age-appropriate. Do let your child know there will be consequences if they willingly watch inappropriate content on their own or with friends.

Encourage Healthy Screen Time Habits

Healthy screen time habits are crucial to maintaining a balanced lifestyle and promoting overall well-being. By setting limits, establishing tech-free zones, and encouraging alternative activities, parents can support tweens in developing healthy habits around screen time and digital device usage. Down below are some advised ways that can assist you with it:

- No screen time after 9 p.m.

- Do not keep smartphones or tablets in the bedroom overnight.

- Help tweens understand how social media affects them mentally, emotionally, and physically.

- Ask questions like "Do you feel you have control over social media, or do you feel like it's controlling you?"

- Encourage tweens to ask: "Do I feel bad about myself while reading someone's social media post?"

Parental Control Apps for Digital Devices

- Track your tween's location by using GPS trackers and apps that can report your tween's location.

- Monitor your tween's use of digital devices via social networks by using Bark or Web Watcher.

- Block websites or filter inappropriate content using the most updated versions built into the device's operating system.

- Use cybersecurity software to detect and warn your tween about suspicious urls.

Manage Digital Devices

- Limit cell phone use during study time or at the dinner table to help tweens take breaks from them.

- Together with your tween, consider turning off notifications from certain apps at specific times each night.

- Model the behavior you expect your child to follow on your digital devices.

- Ask your tween to pay attention to their emotional and physical response when they use their digital devices and when they are not. Ask them questions such as," Does your heart rate increase when your cell phone vibrates?" or "Do you feel bad when you get negative feedback on a post?"

- Request policy information on the use of digital devices from your tween's school.

- Conduct research with your tween on how social media platforms, games, and apps get paid. Discuss why companies might want children and adults to spend more time on their platforms and the tricks they may use to keep your tween's attention.

Encourage More Physical and Outdoor Activities

- Do something fun with your children that involves physical activities, such as playing in the park, playing sports, jogging, hiking, and biking, that they enjoy and naturally require them to be away from their devices.

- If your child is not into sports and exercise, ask them to help with yard work or gardening so they feel a sense of accomplishment and require them to be away from their devices.

- Take your child with you when you're running errands, such as grocery shopping or walking the dog if you have one, etc., that require them to be away from their devices.

- Please encourage your child and their friends to do more outdoor or physical activities during play dates whenever the weather permits.

Key Takeaways:

- Understand the challenges of the digital age.

- Guide your tween to navigate online interactions safely and responsibly.

- Foster digital literacy, resilience, and healthy habits.

- Encourage physical or outdoor activities that take their attention away from their devices.

- Allow tweens to harness the power of technology to enhance their lives and make informed choices online.

As we reflect on the complexities of navigating the digital age, let us remember that with awareness comes empowerment. In the chapters ahead, we'll explore practical strategies for complex circumstances.

PART 5: SPECIAL CONSIDERATIONS FOR COMPLEX CIRCUMSTANCES

Chapter 13: Raising Middle Schoolers During and After a Divorce or Separation

"At the end of the day, the most overwhelming key to a child's success is the positive involvement of the parents."

— *Jane D. Hull*

Raising tweens is a difficult process in itself, and it gets more difficult when parents are going through divorce or separation. Entering middle school is already a big transition for tweens. How can parents help them with additional adjustments at home? To deal with this, let's focus on the following key areas.

Help Your Tween Cope With a Divorce

Despite the scary results like children going through depression, anxiety, attachment issues, or even build-up trauma that most of the research suggests, parents can help their tweens during a divorce to prevent or mitigate these issues.

Below are simple strategies to help your tweens cope with a divorce, provided that you also put what you learned in previous chapters into practice.

- Respond openly and honestly to your child's concerns or questions; you can help them through this difficult time.

- If you are dealing with a difficult ex-partner, attend family and co-parenting therapy with your child and your ex-partner together so your child knows that both parents love your child and have your child's best interest at heart; although parents have different opinions and make different choices in life.

- Reassure your child that not living together as a family does not change your and your ex-partner's parental love for your child.

- Speak in a neutral tone whenever your conversation with your child mentions your ex-partner.

There are many excellent co-parenting resources available. The bottom line is:

1. You and your ex-partner must focus on your child's mental, emotional, and physical well-being as the top priority. Although both parties understand the concept of putting your child's best interest first, we are all humans. It's not easy to put that into practice, especially if your ex did unforgivable things to you and your family. Let's compartmentalize those emotions and focus on your child's well-being.

2. Whenever you get emotional, please revisit Chapter 1 - Self Care to keep you grounded and calm.

3. Make sure neither you nor your ex-partner intentionally or unintentionally weaponize your child against each other during a divorce. Whatever drama happens between two adults should not involve your child.

Understand Your Tween's Perspectives

Divorce can be tumultuous for tweens, triggering confusion and sadness. Understanding their perspective is vital for providing support during this transition. Tweens undergoing significant physical and emotional changes are affected by the additional emotional stress stemming from parental divorce. While many react similarly, cognitive abilities and puberty effects can lead to differing responses. Tweens' involvement in school and hobbies complicates the process. However, with time, children tend to adjust. Co-parents should collaborate to avoid and minimize adding stress for their children.

Emotional Impact on Tweens

Preteens and young adolescents aged 11 to 13 possess a deeper understanding of divorce compared to younger children due to their heightened cognitive abilities. They may grasp the reasons behind divorce and adapt to differing rules in each household, yet may struggle with feelings of depression and self-blame, especially when past and current arguments between you and your ex-partner that your child heard involve how to raise your child.

Some children conceal their distress, appearing indifferent to the absence of one parent to avoid upsetting the other. Others may assume responsibilities to alleviate parental stress or exhibit frustration through rebellious behavior, such as substance use or delinquency.

Additionally, they may develop attachment issues, siding with one parent and rejecting the other. Adolescents at this age increasingly value independence but may fear it due to the perceived permanence of their parents' absence. This may hinder their emotional development and social skills, potentially leading to academic decline and low self-esteem.

Provide Emotional Support

Emotional support plays a crucial role in helping tweens navigate the complexities of divorce. Creating a safe environment for open communication, actively listening to their concerns, and validating their emotions empowers tweens to express themselves and process their feelings healthily. Parents should encourage connections with supportive family and friends, ensuring their tweens feel unconditionally loved and supported.

Offering opportunities for counseling or support groups can also be beneficial. At the same time, parents should seek their support to avoid burdening their tweens. Tweens may experience mixed emotions, including hurt, relief, and anger, especially if they sensed parental unhappiness before the divorce. They may cope by turning to peers, potentially engaging in risky behaviors, highlighting the need for parental guidance, and fostering stronger relationships over time.

Maintain Stability and Routine

Amidst the upheaval of divorce, maintaining stability and routine is essential for providing tweens with a sense of security and predictability. By establishing consistent routines and rituals, parents can help their tweens adjust to their new normal and navigate the changes more easily.

Co-Parent Effectively

Co-parenting is essential for meeting children's needs and maintaining close relationships with both parents unless severe issues like domestic violence or substance abuse are present. The quality of the co-parenting relationship significantly impacts children's mental and emotional well-being.

Despite challenges such as acrimonious splits or contentious relationships, effective co-parenting is achievable with open communication, flexibility, and a shared commitment to prioritizing children's well-being. Overcoming challenges and developing a cooperative co-parenting dynamic enables tweens to thrive in a supportive environment despite the strains of divorce.

Navigate Changes Together

Navigating the changes brought about by divorce demands patience, understanding, and resilience from parents and tweens. Involving tweens in decision-making processes and openly discussing the changes as a family empowers them to navigate transitions with confidence and resilience. Moving, especially with tweens, can evoke sadness or anger about leaving behind friends, schools, and activities. Providing perspective and assuring tweens of ongoing support throughout the transition is crucial.

Preparation is key. Parents should communicate with their tweens beforehand, allowing time to adjust and express emotions. Empathize with their feelings, share your uncertainties, and foster trust and solidarity. Disrupting routines can be incredibly challenging for tweens, who may miss their familiar environment intensely. Parents should validate their emotions, allowing them to process and express feelings through conversation, journaling, or creative outlets. Acknowledging their emotions without trying to alter them reinforces the importance of their feelings and aids in coping with change.

Recognizing that responses vary, parents should offer support tailored to their tween's needs, respecting their unique coping mechanisms. Encouraging tweens to engage in activities that bring comfort and expression fosters emotional well-being. By maintaining open communication, validating emotions, and supporting healthy coping strategies, parents can help their tweens navigate the emotional complexities of divorce and relocation with resilience and understanding.

Tips & Best Practices

1. Keep lines of communication open between parents, caregivers, and children to establish detailed schedules, determine drop-off and pick-up times, and manage expectations.

2. Help children plan for transitions by creating packing lists and sharing plans for visits with caregivers or family members.

3. To help children feel safe and secure, maintain consistent routines, especially during holidays, school breaks, or transitions between households.

4. Make the most of limited time together by minimizing distractions, putting away phones, and focusing on strengthening the parent-child relationship.

5. Although it can be challenging, stay cordial with your ex-partner. Avoid and minimize arguing with your ex-partner in front of your children, no matter how angry or frustrated you are, if your ex-partner fails to bring your child home on time, for example. Practice self-care and self-regulation.

Navigate Blended Families, Step-Sibling Rivalry

Blending families can introduce distinctive challenges, particularly in navigating relationships with step-siblings and adapting to new family dynamics. To facilitate a smooth transition, parents must prioritize open communication, establish clear expectations, and foster positive relationships among all family members, including biological and stepchildren.

Consistency in parenting approaches between biological and stepchildren is vital to prevent feelings of unfair treatment and minimize step-sibling rivalry. Unlike the fairy tale character Cinderella, who endured unjust treatment from her stepfamily, modern tweens may not tolerate perceived inequalities. Thus, parents must ensure fairness and understanding within blended families to promote acceptance and cohesion among all members.

Key Takeaways:

- Raising tweens during and after divorce requires patience, empathy, and resilience on your part.

- By understanding their perspective, providing emotional support, maintaining stability, co-parenting effectively, navigating changes together, and fostering positive relationships in blended families, parents can empower their tweens to thrive despite the challenges of divorce.

- Parenting with a blended family can be easy if consistent standards are applied to both biological and stepchildren.

As we reflect on the complexities of raising tweens during and after divorce, let us remember that families can weather even the stormiest transitions with love, patience, and understanding.

CHAPTER 14: RAISING MIDDLE SCHOOLERS WITH SPECIAL LEARNING NEEDS

"Parents of children with special needs create their own world of happiness and believe in things that others cannot yet see."

— Unknown

Raising tweens while parents go through separation can be difficult, but we learned how to tackle it gracefully. Now, let's address parenting middle schoolers with special learning needs and accommodation. According to the U.S. Department of Health and Human Services, 1 in 5 U.S. children between the ages of 3 and 17 has a mental, emotional, behavioral, or developmental disorder. Many resources specialize in raising children with special needs. For parents new to this topic, I want to summarize key challenges and solutions built on previous chapters with some additional quick pointers.

Now, navigating the diverse landscape of children's learning challenges is akin to unraveling a captivating mystery. From attention deficits to unique cognitive styles, each child presents a unique puzzle waiting to be solved. Understanding these hurdles is crucial in crafting tailored learning experiences that unlock their full potential. Let's delve into the intricate web of learning obstacles, exploring strategies and insights to guide us through your child's middle school journey.

Identify Learning Needs & Behavior Issues

Knowing that every child is unique and may have different learning needs and behavior patterns is essential. Sometimes, certain signs might indicate that your tween could benefit from special learning accommodations. Don't panic or jump to conclusions as you review common signs below. When adults go through something emotionally taxing, such as a divorce, we, too, have difficulty focusing, but it doesn't mean we all have ADHD. Please take a deep breath; let's go through these signs to look out.

- **Difficulty Focusing:** If your tween consistently struggles to pay attention for extended periods or frequently gets distracted, it could be a sign of Attention Deficit Hyperactivity Disorder (ADHD). Tweens with ADHD find it hard to focus and sit still. They might be easily distracted and struggle to follow instructions or finish tasks.

- **Sensory Sensitivities:** Some tweens may be overly sensitive to sights, sounds, textures, or smells. They might cover their ears in noisy environments or avoid certain clothing textures. These sensitivities could be signs of Sensory Processing Disorder (SPD).

- **Emotional & Social Challenges:** If your tween has difficulty making friends, understanding social cues, expressing emotions, and dealing with changes in routine, it could be a sign of autism spectrum disorder (ASD). Autism affects how tweens communicate and interact with others. Your child may also be overly sensitive to normal stimuli, prefer solitary, and have a stronger attachment to objects.

- **Reading Difficulties:** Dyslexia is a common learning difference that affects reading fluency and comprehension. Your tween might struggle with decoding words, recognizing sight words, and understanding written instructions. Dyslexia makes reading challenging. Your tween might struggle with spelling, mix up letters, or have trouble sounding out words.

- **Writing Challenges:** Dysgraphia is a learning disability that affects writing abilities. Your tween may have messy handwriting, difficulty organizing thoughts on paper, and need help with spelling and grammar. Your tween might have messy handwriting, trouble organizing their thoughts on paper, or find it hard to spell words correctly.

- **Poor Coordination:** Some tweens may struggle with fine or gross motor skills, such as tying shoelaces, catching a ball, or using scissors. These challenges could be signs of developmental coordination disorder (DCD).

- **Memory Problems:** If your tween has trouble remembering information, following multi-step instructions, or recalling facts, it might be a sign of a learning disability or attention issues.

- **Emotional Outbursts:** Mood swings, tantrums, and emotional outbursts that seem disproportionate to the situation could be signs of
  underlying stress or frustration related to learning challenges.

Suppose you notice any of these signs in your tween. In that case, seeking guidance
from healthcare professionals, educators, or specialists who can provide assessments and support is essential. Remember, early intervention and tailored accommodations can significantly impact your tween's academic and social success.

Get a Professional Evaluation and Diagnosis

If your tween may need special help with learning or behavior, it's essential to take
steps to get a professional evaluation and diagnosis. Here's what you can do:

- **Talk to Your Pediatrician:** Discuss your concerns with your child's
  pediatrician. They can listen to your observations, ask questions, and
  provide guidance on the next steps. They may also conduct basic screen-
  ings or refer you to specialists for further evaluation.

- **Consult With Educators:** Reach out to your tween's teachers or
  school counselors. They can provide valuable insights into your tween's
  behavior and performance in the classroom. They may also offer sugges-
  tions for support or recommend assessments through the school system.

- **Seek Referrals to Specialists:** Depending on your tween's needs, your
  pediatrician or school professionals may refer you to specialists such
  as psychologists, developmental pediatricians, speech-language pathol-
  ogists, or occupational therapists. These experts can conduct comprehensive evaluations to assess your tween's strengths, challenges, and possible diagnoses. Your family's health insurance usually covers a medical
  specialist visit if the certified professional is inside the insurance coverage
  network.

- **Schedule Assessments:** Schedule appointments with the recommended specialists once you have referrals. Assessments may include interviews, questionnaires, standardized tests, and observations to gather information about your tween's cognitive, social, emotional, and physical
  development.

- **Participate in the Evaluation Process:** During assessments, be open
  and honest about your tween's behaviors, strengths, and challenges.
  Encourage your tween to participate as well, if appropriate, to help
  professionals gain a complete understanding of their needs.

- **Review the Results:** After the evaluations, meet with the specialists to review the findings and discuss any diagnoses or recommendations for support and accommodations. Ask questions and seek clarification to ensure you understand the results fully.

- **Develop a Plan of Action:** Work collaboratively with the professionals involved to develop a personalized action plan for your tween. This plan may include educational accommodations, therapy services, medication options, and home and school support strategies.

Implement Support Strategies

Once you have a plan, take proactive steps to implement the recommended support strategies. Stay in communication with educators, therapists, and healthcare providers to monitor progress and make adjustments as needed.

By seeking professional evaluation and diagnosis, you can ensure that your tween receives the support and accommodations they need to thrive academically, socially, and emotionally. Remember, you're not alone in this journey; resources and professionals are available to help you every step of the way.

Understanding the different types of learning disabilities and challenges can help parents better support their tweens. But don't try to do it all by yourself. Leverage available resources and external help.

Provide Support at Home

1. Create a Structured Environment: Keep things organized at home and school. Use routines and clear expectations to help your tween feel more comfortable and confident.

2. Visual Aids: Use pictures, charts, and schedules to help your tween understand and remember information. Visuals can make learning easier for tweens with learning differences.

3. Hands-On Learning: Get creative with hands-on activities and games. Tweens with learning differences often learn better when they can touch, see, and do things rather than just reading or listening.

4. Encourage Self-Advocacy: Teach your tween to speak up for themselves. Help your child understand their strengths and challenges, and empower them to ask for help when needed.

5. Prioritize Your Self-Care: I can't emphasize this enough. To keep you

calm, centered, and patient, please revisit Chapter 1 on self-care. This will make your life easier and give you more mental, emotional, and physical endurance to support your child with additional learning accommodations better.

Understand Educational Rights and Resources

Understanding the laws and rights that protect tweens with learning needs is essential for ensuring they receive the support they deserve in their education. Here's a simple guide to help you navigate these laws, work with schools to create Individualized Education Programs (IEPs) or 504 Plans, and find resources and support systems for you and your tween.

Educational Laws and Rights

1. Individuals with Disabilities Education Act (IDEA): IDEA is a federal law that ensures children with disabilities have access to a free and appropriate public education (FAPE). Under IDEA, eligible children may receive special education and related services tailored to their needs. These services can include specialized instruction, accommodations, and support services.

2. Section 504 of the Rehabilitation Act: Section 504 prohibits discrimination against individuals with disabilities in federally funded programs, including schools. This law ensures that students with disabilities have equal access to educational opportunities and may receive accommodations and support through a 504 Plan, even if they do not qualify for special education services under IDEA.

Work with Schools to Create an IEP or 504 Plan

Working with schools to create an IEP or 504 plan is equally vital, and here's how you can do it easily.

Identify Your Tween's Needs

Start by gathering information about your tween's learning challenges and strengths. Talk to teachers, specialists, and healthcare providers to identify areas where your tween may need additional support or accommodations.

Request an Evaluation by School

Suppose you suspect that your tween may have a disability that affects their learning. In that case, you can request an evaluation from your tween's school.

These evaluations will assess your tween's educational and developmental needs and determine if they are eligible for special education services under IDEA or accommodations under Section 504.

Attend Meetings and Collaborate

Once the evaluation is complete, you will meet with school staff to discuss the results and develop an appropriate plan for your tween. For an IEP, this plan will outline specific goals, objectives, and services tailored to your tween's needs. For a 504 Plan, the plan will detail accommodations and supports to help your tween access the general education curriculum.

Review and Revise the Plan

It's important to regularly review and update your tween's IEP or 504 Plan to ensure that it continues to meet their evolving needs. Work closely with your tween's teachers and school staff to monitor their progress and make any necessary adjustments to the plan.

Examples of Resources and Support Systems

You can seek further guidance and assistance from some resources and support systems. Some of those resources are:

1. Parent Training and Information Centers (PTIs): PTIs are organizations that provide information, training, and support to parents of children with disabilities. They can help you understand your rights under IDEA and Section 504, navigate the special education process, and connect with other parents facing similar challenges.

2. Local Support Groups: Joining a support group for parents of children with learning needs can provide valuable peer support, advice, and encouragement. These groups often meet regularly to share experiences, resources, and strategies for advocating for their children's education.

3. Online Resources: Many websites and online resources are available to help parents of children with learning needs. Websites like Understood.org, LD.org, and the National Center for Learning Disabilities (NCLD) offer articles, toolkits, webinars, and other resources to help you understand your tween's learning needs and advocate for their education.

4. Professional Help: consult medical professionals, licensed therapists.

If you encounter challenges or difficulties navigating the special education process, consider seeking guidance from an educational advocate, special education attorney, or disability organization. These professionals can provide advice, advocacy, and support to help you ensure that your tween receives the services and accommodations they need to succeed in school.

By understanding your tween's educational rights, working collaboratively with schools to develop appropriate plans, and accessing resources and support systems, you can help them reach their full potential and succeed in their education. Remember, you are not alone in this journey, and many people and organizations are available to support you and your twin every step of the way.

Effective Communication Between Your Child With Educators

Good communication with educators is crucial for tweens because it helps them succeed in school and feel supported. When tweens talk openly with their teachers and school staff, they can share their needs, ask for help when necessary, and build positive relationships that foster a supportive learning environment. Below is why encouraging your tween to communicate directly with educators is essential.

Gain Support and Understanding: When tweens communicate effectively with their educators, they can express their challenges, strengths, and interests. This allows teachers to get first-hand information and provide appropriate support and accommodations tailored to each tween's needs.

Practice Problem-Solving Skills: Open communication enables tweens and educators to work together to solve problems and address concerns. Whether it's difficulty understanding a concept, managing homework, or dealing with social issues, effective communication helps find solutions.

Feel Empowered: When tweens feel comfortable communicating with their educators, they become more empowered in their education. They learn to advocate for themselves, ask questions, and actively participate in their learning journey.

Strategies for Your Child to Effectively Communicate with Educators and Administrators

Now, the question is how to help your tweens converse effortlessly with their educators and administrators. It's easier than you and your tween think.

Be Open and Honest: Encourage your tween to share their thoughts, feelings, and concerns with their educators. Remind them that it's okay to ask for help and that their educators are there to support them.

Establish Regular Communication: Schedule regular check-ins with your tween's teachers to discuss their progress, challenges, and upcoming assignments or projects. This can be done through emails or in-person meetings.

Encourage Active Listening: Teach your tween to listen attentively to their educators and ask clarifying questions. Active listening shows respect and helps both parties understand each other's perspectives.

Use a Communication Notebook: Consider using a communication notebook to exchange messages between home and school. Your tween can use it to jot down questions or concerns, and teachers can use it to provide updates on assignments or classroom activities.

Follow Up: After meetings or discussions with educators, your tween needs to follow up to ensure that any agreed-upon actions or accommodations are being implemented effectively. This demonstrates your tween's commitment to education and can help move the process along.

Tips for You to Advocate for Your Tween's Needs within the School System

There are also some proven and tested tips for advocating for your tweens' needs within their academic curriculum and school system.

1. Know Your Tween's Rights: Familiarize yourself with educational laws and rights, such as IDEA and Section 504, to ensure that your tween receives the support and accommodations they are entitled to.

2. Be Prepared and Organized: Before meetings with educators or school administrators gather relevant documents, such as evaluations, assessments, and previous communication records. This helps you advocate effectively for your tween's needs.

3. Communicate Clearly and Respectfully: When advocating for your tween, be clear and concise in expressing your concerns and desired outcomes. Maintain a respectful and collaborative approach, focusing on finding solutions that benefit your tween.

4. Stay Informed and Engaged: Stay informed about your tween's education by attending school events, volunteering in the classroom, and joining parent-teacher organizations. This allows you to stay engaged in your tween's learning environment and build relationships with school staff.

5. Seek Support: If you encounter challenges or need guidance, don't hesitate to seek support from other parents, professionals, or advocacy groups. These resources can provide valuable advice, encouragement, and strategies for effectively advocating for your tween.

Build a Support Network with Other Parents, Professionals, and Advocacy Groups

- Follow these steps to easily build and establish a support network with other parents, professionals, and advocacy groups.

- Reach out to other parents of children with similar learning needs or challenges. Share experiences, resources, and strategies for supporting your tweens' education.

- Consult with educational advocates, special education attorneys, or disability organizations for guidance and support in navigating the school system and advocating for your tween's needs.

- Consider joining local or online advocacy groups focusing on education and special needs. These groups can provide a platform for sharing information, advocating for policy changes, and connecting with like-minded individuals who share your goals.

- Take advantage of workshops, training, and informational sessions schools, parent organizations, or advocacy groups offer. These events can provide valuable insights, skills, and resources for advocating effectively for your tween.

By prioritizing good communication, advocating for your tween's needs within the school system, and building a solid support network with other parents, professionals, and advocacy groups, you can ensure that your tween receives the support and accommodations they need to succeed in their education. Remember, you are not alone in this journey, and many resources and people are available to support you every step of the way.

Key Takeaways

- Understand different types of learning disability patterns and provide support at home to help your child manage difficulties.

- Effective communication between tweens and educators is essential for success in school and fostering a supportive learning environment.

- Open communication empowers tweens to express their needs, solve problems, and actively participate in their education.

- Strategies for effective communication with educators include being open and honest, establishing regular check-ins, and using communication tools like notebooks.

- Advocating for your tween's needs within the school system involves knowing their rights, being prepared and organized, and communicating clearly and respectfully with educators and administrators at your child's school.

- Build a support network with other parents, professionals, and advocacy groups provides valuable resources, guidance, and encouragement.

- Stay informed, engaged, and proactive is critical to ensuring that your tween receives the support and accommodations they need to succeed in their education.

In this chapter, we have learned about the different kinds of special needs that exist in tweens and discussed strategies and tips for dealing with them accordingly. We also discussed the importance of effective communication between your child and the school as well as between you and the school. The next chapter will focus on homeschooling tweens, which could be an option for middle schoolers with or without special needs.

Chapter 15: Homeschooling Tweens

The first real lesson I learned as a homeschool teacher is that ... it's the students that lead the way."

— *Patti Armstrong*

Whether children have special learning needs or not, homeschooling has become a growing trend among families seeking a tailored and flexible learning environment for their middle schoolers. This approach offers benefits and presents challenges, especially for parents. Let's first look at the key benefits of homeschooling:

- Tailored, individualized learning experience

- One-on-one teaching

- Customized curriculum

- Learning at the child's own pace

- Flexible schedule

- Better accommodation for special learning needs

- Safe and supportive environment

- More bonding time for tweens and parents

- Less peer and social pressures

While homeschooling tweens has plenty of benefits, it can also bring new challenges to the parents. Let's examine common challenges for parents and recommendations to overcome or mitigate these challenges:

More Social Isolation and Less Personal Time: The parent who stays at home feels consumed by homeschooling and caretaking and has little or even less social time or "me time."

Recommendation: You can network and socialize with other homeschooling parents, arrange in-person playdates for your children, or do video chats. You can get your tween involved in community activities so you and your tween can socialize while contributing to your community. Please revisit Chapter 1 and prioritize and carve out time for self-care, no matter how busy you get. If there's a will, there's a way.

Becoming a Full-Time Teacher at Home: Homeschooling involves parents taking on the role of teachers of multiple subjects, which requires spending considerable time planning lessons, supervising activities, and providing one-on-one instruction. You might wonder, "I don't have a teaching degree, and I might remember only a fraction of the content taught in middle school; how can I teach my child when I'm not well-versed in the subject? How much time is that going to take me to learn or relearn the materials and teach my child?"

Recommendation: In previous chapters, we covered cultivating your child's independence, time management, and academic skills; if you have done that foundational work, your teaching job at home can be much easier than you think. You don't have to know everything in the textbooks to guide or supervise your child. Plenty of online instruction videos can assist you and your child.

You might be surprised that providing one-on-one instructions can be more time-efficient for the teacher and the student than sitting in a big classroom. Yes, you're wearing the hat as a teacher, but your instruction time and length are customizable based on your child's and your needs.

Plus, there are curriculum options that some subjects require less hands-on than others. So, take it easy and pace yourself. Seek support when needed; utilize technology, resources, and homeschool parent support groups for proven methods.

Juggling Other Responsibilities: Homeschooling places a significant responsibility on the teaching parent. This can be demanding and time-consuming, especially for parents juggling work and other family responsibilities.

Recommendation: It's admirable that you want to take on such a heavy load. Please be kind to yourself. Reprioritize all the responsibilities on your plate already and get used to saying no to things that are lower priorities. Manage time and resources effectively; prioritize tasks based on importance and urgency, and don't overcommit. Establish clear roles and responsibilities with your spouse/partner — delegate responsibilities at home. Your mental, emotional, and physical well-being directly impacts the quality of homeschooling, your relationship with your child, and the rest of the family.

Your Child Does Not Take Homeschool Seriously: Homeschooling requires parents to create a structured learning environment at home, so when it's education time, your middle schooler takes learning seriously.

Recommendation: Establish schedules and routines, set boundaries, and maintain discipline to ensure your child's learning goals are met and academic progress is achieved. Suppose daily instruction time starts at 9 am. In that case, your middle schooler needs to be ready for learning at 9 am sharp, no different than attending regular schools. If there is no phone usage during class time at regular schools, then the same standard applies to your child at home. Establish schedules and routines and separate personal and school time for you and your middle schooler.

Hard to Switch Between Roles: It could be confusing for parents to be teachers who try to maintain rules and structure for several hours and then switch to loving parents who care for children and play with them.

Recommendation: In addition to establishing the structured learning environment and routines mentioned above, you will want to compartmentalize your thoughts, actions, and emotions to clearly demonstrate your roles to your child at different times of the day.

For example, teachers don't yell or hug a middle schooler inside the classroom when the student gets a poor grade on a test, right? So, during your homeschooling time, you can be compassionate when your child is stuck on math by verbally encouraging him to practice more but don't raise your voice as a disappointed parent or hug your child as an affectionate parent to comfort your child.

Acting like a parent during the instruction period will confuse you and your child, making it harder for you to instill positive discipline in your child. After the instruction period, you can hug your child and tell them you're proud of them for doing more math practice independently.

Curriculum Dilemma: Homeschooling requires access to various educational resources, including textbooks, materials, and online resources, which can be daunting for parents who don't have education degrees or prior teaching experience.

Recommendation: You don't have to start from scratch to create your own curriculum. When you decide to take your child out of their current public school, it's not because the curriculum used at school is terrible, right? You don't have to reinvent the wheel; you can get the same books used at your child's previous school and continue on the same path. You can also access online resources and join homeschool parent groups online or in-person to ask for input. Regardless of which textbooks you use, you will want to ensure the curriculum's scope is at least on par with what's offered at your local schools. Homeschooling is about providing a more suitable learning environment for your child while keeping or improving their academic performance and overall being.

Another consideration factor is the cost of purchasing books and materials. Textbooks, workbooks, and teacher's manuals with answer sheets can get expensive if you add up all the subjects and try to buy them all. So, research and identify textbooks that resonate with you and your child's learning style. And you can always find supplemental online resources to make learning more enjoyable for your child.

Judgment and Unsolicited Advice: It can be disheartening to receive judgment and unsolicited advice from friends and relatives who question the effectiveness of homeschooling or whether your child has enough opportunities to socialize with children in the same age group.

Recommendation: Surround yourself with supportive communities and resources that uplift and validate your decision to homeschool, and remember that, ultimately, you know what's best for your child. Ignore or distance yourself from those nay-sayers, which can be challenging if they are your parents, siblings, or in-laws. You can be firm and polite when you choose to respond, "Thank you for your concern. This is our family decision on what's best for our child."

Regret Giving Up Your Career: It's natural for parents who have invested time and effort into their education and careers to question the sacrifices they make for homeschooling their children. Despite their unwavering love and commitment to their children's well-being, regret and frustration may arise as they navigate the challenges of balancing parenthood and personal aspirations. And sometimes, this regret can transpire into resentment against the working parent with a paid job and possibly a thriving career.

Recommendation: While it's essential to prioritize your children's needs, it's also crucial for you to acknowledge and address your own desires and dreams. You are your child's role model, whether you believe it or not. So, balance nurturing your children's growth and pursuing personal goals. If you constantly wonder what if you go back to the workforce and can use your prior work experience to impact more people's lives, then reevaluate homeschooling. Remember, we tend to think grass is greener on the other side. Many working moms feel guilty when being away from their children for work or business trips. There's no right or wrong answer here. Finding work and life balance is a lifelong journey. Do what feels suitable for you and your family, and allow that feeling to evolve.

By addressing common homeschooling pain points and implementing effective strategies for overcoming challenges, parents can easily create a supportive and enriching learning environment for their tweens. Next, let's discuss systematic approaches to homeschooling:

Set Educational Goals

Before embarking on homeschooling, it's crucial to define clear educational goals. Start by determining which subjects are priorities and set proficiency expectations. Identify critical skills, values, and character traits you aim to foster, such as critical thinking and social-emotional growth.

Tailor education to your child's interests, strengths, and learning styles, adapting teaching methods and curriculum accordingly. Also, envision how homeschooling aligns with broader aspirations for your child's academic and personal success. These considerations ensure a well-rounded educational journey that supports your child's needs and future endeavors.

Create a Supportive Homeschooling Environment

Creating a supportive homeschooling environment that fosters learning and curiosity is essential for your child's educational success and well-being. And it will also make your homeschooling job easier. Here are some tips to help you cultivate a positive and engaging homeschooling environment as parents:

- Establish a dedicated learning space, not next to toys and devices

- Set a sustainable routine

- Encourage exploration and curiosity

- Promote independence, self-learning

- Celebrate achievements, small or big

- Emphasize lifelong learning with your child, no matter what career they end up pursuing

Understand Your Tween's Learning Needs

Identifying your tween's learning style and interests is a crucial step for parents in tailoring their educational experience to maximize engagement and learning. By understanding how your tween learns best and what subjects or activities they are passionate about, you can create a customized learning plan that caters to their needs and preferences. Here're the steps to identify your middle schooler's learning style and interests:

- **Observe and Interact:** Spend time observing how your tween approaches learning tasks and engages with different activities. Pay attention to their preferences for visual, auditory, or hands-on learning experiences.

- **Ask Questions:** Talk to your tween about their interests, hobbies, and favorite subjects. Ask them what topics they enjoy learning about and how they prefer to learn new information.

- **Experiment with Different Approaches:** Try out different teaching methods and activities to see what resonates most with your tween. Offer various learning opportunities, such as reading, watching educational videos, conducting experiments, or participating in hands-on projects.

- **Seek Feedback:** Encourage your tween to provide feedback on their learning experiences. Ask them what they enjoy most about specific activities and what they find challenging or uninteresting.

- **Involve Your Child in the Planning Process:** Once you've identified your tween's learning style and interests, engaging them in the planning process is vital to nurturing independence and motivation. Collaboratively set educational goals and objectives with your tween, discussing their academic aspirations and desired learning experiences.

- **Offer Choices and Autonomy in Their Education:** Allow them to select topics of interest, choose activities, and pace their assignments. Involve them in crafting the curriculum, integrating their interests and preferences into the learning plan.

Regular check-ins and reflections help monitor progress, address challenges, and celebrate accomplishments, encouraging your tween to take ownership of their learning journey. This collaborative approach empowers tweens to become active participants in shaping their education, fostering a sense of responsibility and enthusiasm for learning.

Adapt Teaching Methods and Curriculum

As your tween progresses through their developmental stages, it's vital to adjust teaching methods and curriculum to match their evolving needs. Differentiated instruction allows you to cater to your tween's learning styles and pace, providing varying levels of challenge and support. Incorporating hands-on learning experiences adds depth to their education, engaging them in practical applications of knowledge and fostering a deeper understanding of concepts. Flexibility is critical, enabling you to adapt the curriculum to capitalize on your tween's strengths while addressing areas that require additional attention.

Taking a holistic approach to education ensures that your tween's learning extends beyond academics, encompassing social, emotional, and physical development. Encourage exploration of diverse subjects and passions, fostering a well-rounded education that nurtures their potential. By involving your tween in the planning process and promoting autonomy, you empower them to take ownership of their learning journey. This collaborative approach not only enhances engagement but also instills a lifelong love of learning, preparing your tween for success in the future.

Set Realistic Academic and Personal Development Goals

As Chapter 11 - Academic Success Skills discusses, setting realistic academic and personal developmental goals is essential. Below is a quick recap:

- Collaborate with your tween on goal-setting

- Be specific with goals

- Ensure the goals are measurable, relevant, and time-bound

- Focus on progress

- Don't aim for perfection

- Adjust when required

Balance Parental Supervision and Tween Independence

Gradually increase your tween's independence and autonomy as they demonstrate responsibility and maturity. Provide opportunities for them to take ownership of their learning and make decisions about their daily routine. Set clear expectations and guidelines for your tween regarding their responsibilities, behavior, and academic performance. Communicate openly and regularly about your expectations and offer support and guidance as needed.

Maintain open lines of communication with your tween to address any concerns, questions, or challenges. Please encourage them to voice their opinions, share their ideas, and express their needs. At the same time, monitor your tween's progress and check in regularly to review their work, provide feedback, and offer assistance as needed. Offer praise and encouragement to reinforce positive behavior and academic achievements.

Incorporate Social and Extracurricular Activities

Incorporating social and extracurricular activities into homeschooling is essential for fostering social interactions, building friendships, and providing opportunities for real-world learning experiences. Parents can create a rich and diverse learning environment beyond the traditional school setting by leveraging homeschool networks, online communities, and local resources. Here are examples of exploring extracurricular activities and real-world learning:

- **Field Trips and Excursions:** Plan regular field trips and excursions to museums, zoos, botanical gardens, historical sites, and other educational destinations. These outings provide hands-on learning experiences and opportunities for children to explore new interests and topics outside the classroom.

- **Outdoor Adventures:** Take advantage of nature's classroom by incorporating outdoor activities such as hiking, camping, gardening, and nature walks into your homeschooling routine. Outdoor adventures promote physical activity, environmental awareness, and appreciation for the natural world.

- **Cultural Experiences:** Expose your child to diverse cultures and traditions through cultural festivals, ethnic restaurants, and cultural events in your community. Immersing children in different cultures broadens their perspective, fosters empathy, and promotes cultural understanding.

- **Internships and Apprenticeships:** Explore internship or apprenticeship opportunities for older tweens to gain real-world experience in a field of interest. Whether shadowing a professional, volunteering at a local business, or completing a hands-on project, internships provide valuable hands-on learning experiences and insights into potential career paths.

- **Online Learning Platforms:** Take advantage of online learning platforms and educational resources to supplement your homeschooling curriculum. From virtual classes and webinars to interactive games and educational videos, online platforms offer many resources to enhance learning and engage children in meaningful ways. Of course, you also need to remind your middle schooler to keep total screen time within reason.

- **Connect with Online Communities:** Join homeschooling forums, social media groups, and online communities to connect with other homeschooling families, share resources, and exchange ideas. Online communities provide a valuable source of support, encouragement, and practical advice for homeschooling parents.

- **Utilize Local Resources:** Explore local libraries, museums, science centers, and community centers that offer homeschool programs, workshops, and events. These institutions often provide special discounts or free admission for homeschoolers and host educational activities tailored to homeschooling families.

Attend Homeschool Conferences and Events

Attend homeschool conferences, workshops, and conventions in your area to network with other homeschooling parents, discover new curriculum options, and gain insights into homeschooling best practices. These events offer opportunities for learning, inspiration, and connecting with like-minded families.

Participate in Community Events

Please get involved in community events, festivals, and fairs that offer opportunities for children to showcase their talents, skills, and interests. Whether it's a science fair, art exhibition, or talent show, community events provide platforms for children to shine and connect with their community.

Use Technology and Resources to Supplement

Recommendations for educational technology tools, online resources, and homeschooling apps can significantly enhance the learning experience for both parents and tweens. By leveraging these resources effectively, parents can provide engaging and interactive learning opportunities that complement their homeschooling curriculum.

There are many excellent educational tools and online resources that can enrich your child's education experience, knowledge, and skills. You can experiment and see which best meets your child's learning needs, such as Khan Academy,

Duolingo, Scratch, PBS Learning Media, Quizlet, Reading Eggs, IXL, BrainPOP, Adventure Academy, Prodigy, etc.

Prepare For High School & Beyond

Planning for the transition to high school is an important step in your tween's educational journey, whether they continue homeschooling or transition to traditional school settings. When going through such a transition, consider the educational options available for high school, including continuing homeschooling, enrolling in a traditional public or private school, or exploring hybrid programs. Assess your tween's academic needs, preferences, and goals to determine the best fit.

Remember to research the admission requirements, curriculum offerings, extracurricular activities, and support services available at potential high schools. Attend open houses, tour campuses, and meet with school administrators to gather information and ask questions. After that, ensure your tween is academically prepared for the rigors of high school coursework by reviewing prerequisite subjects, strengthening foundational skills, and exploring advanced placement or honors courses if applicable.

While going through the process, provide emotional support and guidance to help your tween successfully navigate the transition to high school. Encourage open communication, address any concerns or anxieties they may have, and emphasize the opportunities for growth and development that lie ahead.

Explore Career and Vocational Interests

While going through such a big transition, it is also important to know what your child is interested in and then look into career exploration accordingly. Now, while helping them understand their interest and letting them explore options, focus on these guidelines as they can help you profoundly as a parent:

1. Help your tween identify their strengths, interests, and passions through self-reflection, personality assessments, and exploration of potential career paths. Please encourage them to pursue activities and experiences that align with their interests and goals.

2. Research various career fields, industries, and occupations to expand your tween's awareness of potential career opportunities. Explore online resources, informational interviews, job shadowing opportunities, and career exploration programs to learn more about different career paths.

3. Encourage your tween to explore different vocational interests through

hands-on experiences, internships, part-time jobs, or volunteer work. Exposure to real-world environments can help them gain valuable skills, clarify their career goals, and make informed decisions about their future.

4. Offer support and guidance as your tween navigates career exploration and decision-making. Help your middle schooler set realistic goals, develop action plans, and seek out mentors or advisors who can offer guidance and advice. That's how you can help your tweens step into different stages of life without any hurdles and stress.

Be Flexible about Homeschooling Decision

Many parents struggle with homeschooling but want to continue doing so simply because they want to avoid feeling guilty for returning their children to public schools.

1. Do not feel guilty because you are human, and humans have physical limitations, even for those who seem to live charmed lives.

2. If you have done everything you could and are still struggling, my best tip for you now is not to try to force a square peg into a round hole. Homeschooling is not for everyone. Take the path of less resistance to prioritize your well-being, which directly impacts your child's well-being.

3. As discussed in Chapter 4, helping your child build resilience is the same principle that applies to you as a parent. Treat each failure as a lesson in life. Learn from it, but don't dwell on it. Your success or failure in homeschooling does not define who you are as a parent.

4. What seemed to be a good decision when you decided to homeschool may or may not be the optimal decision now. It does not mean that you were wrong in the past. If you're struggling with homeschooling, it's a sign that you need to focus on the present and all the options.

You probably have heard the saying, "Happy wife, happy home." Well, it's equally true: happy parents, happy children. If you're unhappy, your child will be impacted by negative emotions.

Key Takeaways:

1. Understand homeschooling benefits.

2. Understand homeschooling challenges for parents and apply the recommendations to mitigate and overcome these challenges.

3. Create a supportive homeschooling environment and understand your tweens' learning needs.

4. Set realistic academic and personal development goals with your tween.

5. Adapt teaching methods and leverage available resources.

6. Consider various ideas in this chapter to promote and facilitate your tween's social interactions.

7. Prepare your tween for high school and beyond, and encourage them to do what interests them.

8. Be flexible about your homeschooling decision and be kind to yourself.

All the insights, recommendations, and tips covered in this chapter should help make homeschooling easier and more manageable if you decide to take this journey with your child.

CONCLUSION

In this comprehensive guidebook for parents of tweens who attend middle school, we've explored a range of topics aimed at helping you nurture their growth and development during this crucial stage of life with proven strategies and tips for making your parenting journey easier. Let's recap the key themes and learnings from each of these areas:

- **Prioritize Your Self-Care:** As parents, it's vital to prioritize self-care to maintain physical, emotional, and mental well-being. By caring for ourselves, we're better equipped to effectively support and care for our tweens.

- **Understand Your Tween:** Understanding your tween's unique needs, interests, and developmental stages is essential for fostering a supportive and nurturing environment. By recognizing their individuality, we can tailor our approach to parenting and education accordingly.

- **Empower Your Tween with Self-Care:** Teach your tween the importance of self-care practices such as healthy habits, stress management techniques, and seeking support when needed. Empowering them to take care of themselves builds resilience and promotes overall well-being.

- **Foster Independence:** Encouraging independence in tweens fosters confidence, self-reliance, and problem-solving skills. By gradually giving them opportunities to make decisions and take responsibility for their actions, we empower them to navigate the world confidently.

- **Build Resilience and Flexibility:** Life is full of ups and downs, and teaching tweens resilience and flexibility equips them with the skills to adapt and bounce back from challenges. Please encourage them to embrace change, learn from setbacks, and maintain a positive outlook.

- **Stress Management and Mental Self-Care:** Equip tweens with effective stress management techniques and strategies for maintaining mental well-being. Teach them mindfulness, relaxation techniques, and healthy coping mechanisms to navigate stress and anxiety.

- **Cultivate Emotional Intelligence and Effective Communication:** Help tweens develop emotional intelligence by effectively recognizing and managing their emotions. Encourage open communication, empathy, and active listening skills to foster healthy relationships and resolve conflicts.

- **Establish Social Skills and Healthy Relationships:** Guide tweens in developing social skills, including empathy, respect, and cooperation. Encourage positive peer interactions, teach them to set boundaries, and support them in building healthy relationships.

- **Acquire Essential Life Skills:** Introduce tweens to essential life skills such as healthy cooking, staying safe, financial literacy, problem-solving, decision-making, and critical thinking. These skills are crucial for navigating adulthood and achieving success in various aspects of life.

- **Learn Time Management and Goal Setting:** Model effective time management and goal-setting behaviors for tweens to emulate. Teach them to prioritize tasks, set SMART goals, and manage their time effectively to achieve academic and personal success.

- **Develop Academic Success Skills:** Support tweens in developing academic skills such as organization, study habits, and time management. Provide resources, guidance, and encouragement to help them excel academically and reach their full potential.

- **Navigate the Digital Age:** Educate tweens about responsible digital citizenship, online safety, and healthy technology use. Set clear guidelines and boundaries for screen time, monitor their online activities, and teach them to use technology responsibly.

- **Raise Tweens Amidst Separation:** Offer support and reassurance to tweens experiencing family separation or divorce. Create a safe and stable environment, encourage open communication, and allow them to express their feelings and concerns.

- **Raise Tweens Who Need Special Learning Accommodations:** Advocate for your tween's unique learning needs and provide the necessary support and accommodations to help them succeed academically. Collaborate with educators, seek specialized services, and celebrate their achievements.

- **Homeschooling Tweens:** If you decide to homeschool tweens, apply the recommendations to overcome challenges stemming from your worries and concerns. Then, create a supportive and enriching learning environment tailored to your child's needs and interests. Utilize educational resources, technology, and homeschooling community support. Celebrate your child's progress and accomplishments. Be flexible about your homeschooling decision.

In summary, raising tweens is a multifaceted journey filled with challenges, joy, and growth opportunities. When prioritizing self-care and understanding changes your tween experiences while entering puberty and attending middle school, you are laying a solid foundation for yourself to tackle any parenting challenges. By helping your child develop independence, build resilience, and manage stress, you empower your child with self-confidence. As you guide your child to develop emotional intelligence, effective communication, and social skills, they become more self-sufficient in navigating complex interactions and building meaningful relationships inside and outside school, making your parenting job easier. As you guide and support your child in time management, goal-setting, academic success, and navigating the digital age, you further empower your child to thrive in school and beyond. Life is filled with exciting twists and turns. Strategies and tips for tackling special circumstances further equip you to handle new challenges due to new life situations with confidence and ease.

Congratulations on completing this book! This is already a massive step towards blissful parenting. Treat this book as your daily guide and companion, and believe that parenting middle schoolers will get easier as you apply the strategies and tips covered in the book. You are welcome to customize some approaches to address your unique situations. Applying only a subset of the solutions and tips will make parenting your middle schooler easier.

Get the Audio Format as Your Daily Companion

I want to make this journey as easy as possible for you. This book is also available in audio format, allowing you to listen to the content on the go or during relaxation. You can get the audiobook by scanning the QR code below.

Your Voice Matters! Your Rating/Review Can Empower Other Parents

Leaving a rating/review of this book on Amazon is quick and easy. Scan the QR code below now.

Thank you for being part of this parenting support circle. ere's to the joyful and fulfilling parenting journey!

- Your parenting friend and cheerleader, Grace A. Clark

REFERENCES

- Olson, E. MD. (2023, February 21). *How Many Hours of Sleep Are Enough?* Mayo Clinic. https://www.mayoclinic.org/healthy-lifestyle/adult-health/expert-answers/how-many-hours-of-sleep-are-enough/faq-20057898

- Smith, M., MA. (2024, February 5). *Social Support for Stress Relief.* HelpGuide.org. https://www.helpguide.org/articles/stress/social-support-for-stress-relief.htm

- Fisher, T. (2024, January 5). *The 9 Best Android Emulators for Windows 10 and Windows 11.* Lifewire. https://www.verywellfamily.com/how-to-teach-time-management-skills-to-teens-4175015

- Finn, J. (2020, February 1). *Goal-Setting for Tweens: Here's What to Know.* TODAY.com. https://www.today.com/parenting-guides/goal-setting-tweens-t177664

- Baum, R. MD & Shahidullah, J. PhD. (n.d.). *Teaching Time Management to Teens: Less Stress, More Balance.* HealthyChildren.org. https://www.healthychildren.org/English/family-life/family-dynamics/Pages/time-management-as-a-teen-wellness-tool-less-stress-more-balance.aspx

- Tillman, V. (2021, November 29). *Help Your Teen Create SMART Goals.* 7sistershomeschool.com. https://www.7sistershomeschool.com/help-your-teen-create-smart-goals

- Yourtherapysource. (2022, August 11). *SMART Goals for Teens.* Your

Therapy Source. https://www.yourtherapysource.com/blog1/2022/0 8/11/smart-goals-for-teens-3

- Morin, A. (n.d.). *How to Help Teens Develop Good Study Habits*. Understood. https://www.understood.org/en/articles/how-to-help-your-tee n-develop-good-study-habits

- Sim. (2024, Feb 9). *Ways to Help Teenagers Overcome Academic Challenges*. Sim's Life. https://simslife.co.uk/help-teenagers-overcome-aca demic-challenges

- Austin, A. (2023, August 15). *5 Tips to Help Your Teen Plan for Their Future*. Connections Academy. https://www.connectionsacademy.com/support/resources/article /5-tips-for-helping-teens-plan-ahead-for-a-sizzling-future

- Lee, N. (2023, August 11). *Parenting in the Digital Age: Navigating Challenges*. The ARKGroup. https://thearkgroup.org/parenting-in-t he-digital-age-navigating-challenges

- Pearson, C. (2023, May 23). *Helping Teens With Social Media - How Parents Can Actually Help Teens Navigate Social Media*. NY Times. https://www.nytimes.com/2023/05/15/well/family/kids-soci al-media.html

- Feinberg, M. E., Kan, M. L., & Hetherington, E. M. (2007). *The Longitudinal Influence of Coparenting Conflict on Parental Negativity and Adolescent Maladjustment*. Journal of Marriage and the Family, *69*(3), 687–702. https://doi.org/10.1111/j.1741-3737.2007.00400.x

- Wallace, L. & Sparks K. (2016, April). *Helping Preteens and Adolescents Adjust to Divorce*. MU Extension. https://extension.missouri.edu/pub-lications/gh6616

Made in United States
Orlando, FL
01 June 2025

61780182R00070